Explore
COLORADO

Explore COLORADO

A Naturalist's Notebook

BY Frances Alley Kruger AND Carron A. Meaney

PHOTOGRAPHY BY John Fielder

Denver Museum of Natural History AND Westcliffe Publishers

The Denver Museum of Natural History appreciates the support of the following individuals and organizations, who helped make this book possible:

Valerie Gates, Carlye Wattis, Bureau of Land Management,

AND

Stanley and Deborah Loftness, Charles and Barbara Miller,
Mary Ann and Harold Norblom, and Bob and Cindy Sestrich

International Standard Book Number: 1-56579-124-X

Library of Congress Catalog Number: 95-60670

Copyright © Denver Museum of Natural History, 1995.

All rights reserved.

Published by the Denver Museum of Natural History and
Westcliffe Publishers, 2650 South Zuni Street, Englewood,
Colorado 80110

Printed in Hong Kong by Palace Press International

No portion of this book, either photographs or text, may
be reproduced in any form without the written permission
of the publishers.

The Museum's programs and exhibits are made
possible in part by funds from the Scientific and
Cultural Facilities District.

ACKNOWLEDGMENTS

BOOK PROJECT MANAGER: Betsy R. Armstrong

GRAPHIC DESIGNER: Ann W. Douden

ILLUSTRATORS: Jackie McFarland, Steve Elliot,
    Elizabeth Biesiot, Dick Hanna

PHOTOGRAPHERS: John Fielder; Wendy Shattil and
    Robert Rozinski; Denver Museum of Natural History
    photography: Nancy Jenkins, Rick Wicker,
    Gary Hall, Richard Stum, David McGrath

EDITOR: Karen M. Nein

PROOFREADER: Laurie Rogers

ASSISTANTS: James T. Alton, Danielle Okin

SCIENTIFIC REVIEWERS: Allen Crockett,
    Audrey Benedict

ECOSYSTEM CONSULTANTS: David Cooper,
    John Emerick, David Armstrong

(preceding page) Pawnee Buttes, Pawnee National Grassland

(right) Beaver ponds, Sawatch River

To My Inspirations,

Steve, Rebecca, and

Joshua

F.K.

For Mara

C.M.

Gunnison National

Forest

Contents

Preface 8

Introduction to Colorado's Ecosystems 10

Grassland 22

Semidesert Shrubland 32

Piñon-Juniper Woodland 42

Riparian Land 52

Montane Shrubland 62

Montane Forest 72

Subalpine Forest 82

Treeline 92

Alpine Tundra 102

Activities for All Seasons 112

Bibliography and Suggested Reading 122

Photography and Illustration Credits 124

Index 126

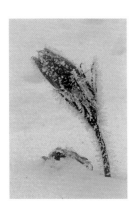

Pasque flower in
the snow

*M*ost of all, the authors would like to acknowledge our debt to the work of those who came before us. In writing this book, we are undoubtedly "standing on the shoulders of giants." The classic work of C. Hart Merriam on lifezones, for instance, has served as the ultimate springboard for all later work on ecosystems.

The Denver Museum of Natural History dioramas—life-size recreations of scenes from nature—are among the best in the world. Most of them were originally created in the 1930s. They feature the work of such renowned artists and naturalists as Waldo Love, background painter extraordinaire, and Alfred M. Bailey and Robert Neidrach, larger-than-life Museum legends. Some of the illustrations in this book, in fact, are the work of Dr. Bailey. During the 1930s, the Museum's "Accessories Department," where the foreground plants for the dioramas were made, was staffed with artisans from the Works Progress Administration (WPA). During the Great Depression, the WPA provided a variety of jobs for many such people, whose work has left an enduring legacy nationwide. At the Denver Museum of Natural History, in 1937 alone, these wonder workers produced some 56,000 leaves and 5,000 flowering stalks!

By the time the 1990s rolled around, the Walter C. Mead Colorado Ecological Hall, where most of the dioramas pictured in this book are located, was in serious need of a face-lift. Carron Meaney, then curator of mammalogy at the Museum, had been attracted for many years by the prospect of reinterpreting the hall and had a great desire to respond to the challenge. Frances Kruger, exhibit developer and interpretive writer, had been thinking about user-friendly ways to write new labels and to reinterpret old exhibit halls. A partnership was born, and in 1991 the

Cobwebs

Museum reopened the revitalized hall as *Explore Colorado: From Plains to Peaks.* This book is the natural extension of our work (and fun!) together on the exhibit hall—a way for you to take it home with you, and even out on the road.

As part of an ongoing interest in Colorado's biodiversity (the number and variety of plants and animals that live in a given place) and as part of the research for the *Explore Colorado* exhibition, Dr. Meaney brought together a group of local scientists. Together they developed a new ecosystem classification for Colorado. David Armstrong and John Emerick were especially helpful. David Cooper was a true working partner in defining and mapping the ecosystems. His understanding of Colorado plants and active participation in fieldwork were essential to the project.

Prairie coneflower

For a book like this, what better photographer to bring Colorado's ecosystems to life in all seasons than John Fielder? In the minds of many who know the state only from afar, Fielder's photographs ARE Colorado. The fine work of wildlife photographers Wendy Shattil and Robert Rozinski is, appropriately, also featured. Artists Steve Elliott, Jackie McFarland, and Elizabeth Biesiot, book designer Ann Douden, and champion assistants James Alton and Danielle Okin have all contributed their talents.

We would also like to thank Audrey Benedict, herself an author and expert on Colorado's ecosystems, for her thoughtful and timely review of the words and examples in this book, and Allen Crockett, for reviewing countless illustrations.

Enjoy!

A first-time visitor to Denver was heard to say, "It's so <u>flat</u>! I thought Colorado was covered with mountains!" When newcomers drive into Colorado from the east, they may think they're still in Kansas. Driving in from the west, they might swear they're still in Utah. And they'd almost be right! Parts of Colorado look very different from each other— but a lot like their neighboring states. Going from east to west, Colorado is roughly one-third high plains, one-third mountains, and one-third canyon country.

People often drive long distances in Colorado to get from one place to another. Do you look out your car windows and watch the world go by when you travel? It's hard not to.

The plains seems to stretch for miles. There's not a tree in sight. It sure seems empty. This trip is taking forever. Look, the mountains are up ahead at last! And there are a few trees over by that dry streambed. Now we just have to get through Denver . . . buildings and people everywhere. Whew! Now the landscape is starting to get interesting—some scattered trees and shrubby-looking plants along these foothills. Aaah—the mountains at last. Trees everywhere, cliffs and canyons, and the sound of water. Soon we'll be up on top of the world!

Treeless City, USA

Did you know that if it weren't for human intervention—in the form of planting and watering—Denver wouldn't have any trees at all (except for a few cottonwoods along the banks of rivers and streams)? Denver is a plains city, and the plains are too dry for most trees to grow.

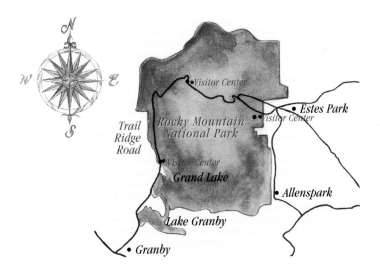

Trail Ridge Road is the highest continuous paved highway in the world and winds its way to an elevation of over 12,000 feet between the east and west sides of Rocky Mountain National Park. Snow, wind, and cold close the road in winter, but it reopens each year around Memorial Day.

For every 1,000-foot rise in elevation, the average temperature drops by about 3 degrees Fahrenheit. Above 9,000 feet, frost is possible any night of the year—even in midsummer.

What you see as you travel through Colorado is what a naturalist sees: evidence of biodiversity. More different environments are found here, and more different plants and animals, than in most other states. In fact, a 100-mile drive from Denver to the top of Trail Ridge Road in Rocky Mountain National Park takes you through similar environments—with many of the same plants and animals—that you would find on a 1,500-mile journey north to the Arctic.

Colorado's dramatic contours shape its character. Elevation—height above sea level—has a lot to do with what an area is like. The Rocky Mountains, thrusting skyward along a north-south spine through the center of Colorado, separate the grasslands of the eastern plains from the canyon country of western Colorado.

From just over 3,000 feet above sea level at Holly on the eastern plains to more than 14,400 feet at the top of Mount Elbert, there is a difference of more than 11,000 vertical feet!

Colorado's mountains influence how wet or dry different parts of the state are—and even affect the "how, when, and where" of rain- and snowfall. The western third of Colorado is very dry, usually receiving only what moisture falls there as snow in the winter. The grassy, eastern part of Colorado is dry, too, getting mostly spring and summer moisture—the product of upslope storms from the east and afternoon thunderstorms that manage to cross the mountains. The mountains, of course, get more moisture than any other part of the state, in both winter and summer.

North America's prevailing winds blow from west to east. Moisture is much more likely to precipitate out of clouds when they pass over the mountains than it is before or after.

Mountains even determine local wind patterns. In the morning, cool air drains from the mountainsides, causing winds to blow down-valley. Later in the day, as the mountainsides heat up, rising warm air causes up-valley winds.

Early morning

Late afternoon

Colorado's famous chinook winds are strong, gusty, and, most of all, WARM. The name comes from the northwest coast Chinook Indians, who called warm winds off the Pacific Ocean "snow eaters." Mild winds from the Pacific bring Colorado its chinooks, too. The warm, westerly air is forced up and over the mountains. Under certain conditions, the air continues to ripple up and down to the east of the Rockies. The air speeds up, and gets even warmer, as it rides these "mountain waves" eastward.

Obviously, Colorado's mountains have a major effect on both temperature and moisture throughout the state. But many other things also work together to determine what lives where. Juggle the factors of elevation, temperature, moisture, sunshine, wind, soil, and steepness in different combinations, and you get a framework of environmental conditions—each supporting its own kinds of plants. Groups of plants, in turn, provide varied habitats for different kinds of animals.

*A*pplying names (or any other set of categories and definitions) to different parts of the land (or to anything else) is a peculiarly human activity. It gives people a way to think about things. As more is observed and learned, names and categories change—giving people new ways to appreciate and understand. Observation, study, classification and more observation, more study, and reclassification are part of the study of nature.

Ever since the mid-1800s when botanists and zoologists began to investigate the Rocky Mountain West, scientists have devised various ways to classify its land, plants, and animals. One such system that many people are familiar with is the "lifezone" concept. This approach named different parts of the land based on elevation, dividing it into a series of seven clearly defined horizontal bands across the mountains.

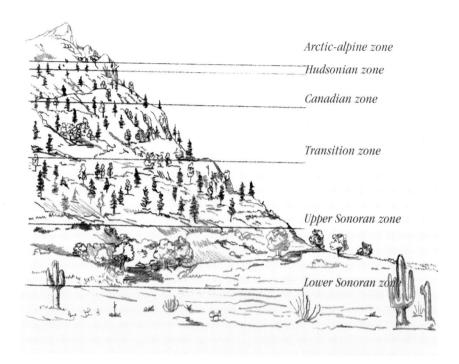

Arctic-alpine zone

Hudsonian zone

Canadian zone

Transition zone

Upper Sonoran zone

Lower Sonoran zone

Lifezones were an instructive idea that helped shape the way people thought about the western landscape. They were the first step in defining the patterns of nature in the West. In a broad sense, the principles of the lifezone system still hold true. But nothing is ever really quite that simple, and in the past hundred years people have learned a lot more about the western landscape.

"Lifezones" in the mountain west were first defined by C. Hart Merriam in 1890. The system was later refined by many different biologists, eventually taking the form of this familiar diagram of horizontal bands.

Remember the view from your car windows when you drive through the mountains? The sights you see are more likely to form organic, zigzag, or mosaic patterns than they are to look like horizontal bands. Nor do you always find forests above shrublands, shrublands above grasslands, and grasslands above deserts.

Today's approach looks at dynamic ecosystems. An ecosystem is a recognizable grouping of plants, animals, environmental conditions, and the interactions among them. How big is an ecosystem? Well, size is in the mind of the speaker—an ecosystem could be as big as the Rocky Mountains or as small as a square foot of soil, containing a single kind of plant and one or two animals. Some scientists have divided the state into as many as 33 separate categories.

In the Northern Hemisphere, north-facing slopes get less sun than south-facing slopes. Temperatures are therefore lower and moisture levels higher on northern exposures. You could say that different habitats exist from one side of the valley to another.

When the Denver Museum of Natural History began the task of renovating and reinterpreting its Colorado Ecological Hall in 1991, local scientists, led by Museum zoologist Carron Meaney, took another look at how we think about Colorado. They came up with a simplified classification system of the major ecosystems. Their goal was to develop a system that is easy to use and scientifically valid. The resulting eight ecosystems are defined largely by their dominant plants.

In 1991, the Denver Museum of Natural History developed a simple yet accurate approach to classifying Colorado's ecosystems. The eight ecosystems have familiar, descriptive names and reflect the realities of nature and of Colorado's topography.

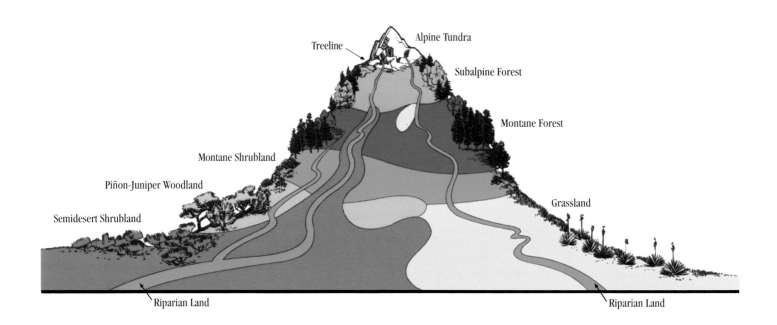

Denver Museum of Natural History zoologist Carron Meaney, shown here, and plant ecologist David Cooper traveled the state—collecting data and observing changes in vegetation—to create this new ecosystem map.

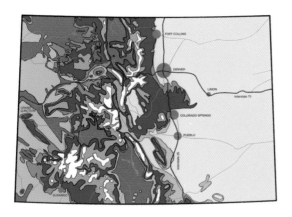

Colorado's Ecosystems

The new eight-ecosystem classification developed at the Denver Museum of Natural History has been adopted by the Bureau of Land Management, Rocky Mountain National Park, Jefferson County Parks and Recreation, and the Colorado Division of Wildlife, among others. More organizations and individuals are using it all the time. We hope that you find it understandable and easy to use—and that it gives you new ways to think about what you see around you.

Confused about plant names? So is everybody!

Scientific names are given to all plants and animals; they pinpoint where an organism fits into our classification of the natural world. The first word in a scientific name is the genus name, the second is the species name. Sometimes there is a third, or subspecies, name. Scientific names are always in Latin.

The plant names used in this book and in the Denver Museum of Natural History's *Explore Colorado* exhibition follow the nomenclature of William Weber in his books, published in 1987 and 1990, on the flora of Colorado's eastern and western slopes. In this nomenclature, some familiar genus names have been changed. A citation like *Sabina (=Juniperus) monosperma* means that the current genus *Sabina* used to be called *Juniperus*. The species name, *monosperma*, remains the same. Dr. Weber is a professor emeritus of botany at the University of Colorado in Boulder. He has spent a lifetime studying the flora of Colorado and works in the herbarium at the University of Colorado Museum.

Yucca

Some plants are found in many different places and play a role in several ecosystems. Aspens, Douglas-firs, lodgepole pines, sagebrush, and yuccas are among the plants you'll find in more than one ecosystem.

The same is true of animals. Some, such as mule deer and coyotes, roam widely. Others, such as pikas and piñon jays, are tied to just one kind of environment.

Pika

Like workers who have a broad set of general skills, plants and animals that can—and do—live in lots of different places are considered generalists. Other species are specialists, with narrower, more focused abilities. Specialists that thrive only in a particular environment have adapted—sometimes in dramatic or bizarre ways—to the conditions there.

We hope that this book inspires you to enjoy and examine Colorado's landscapes—whether from your armchair, through your car windows, or along a backcountry trail—and that it gives you new tools for experiencing the naturalist's thrill of recognizing plants, animals, and interactions for yourself.

If, one day, you find yourself saying,

Camouflaged to change color along with the changing seasons

Ptarmigan in winter white

The saguaro cactus of Arizona and Mexico is adapted for storing water to live in the dry, sunny desert.

Abert's squirrel

Those trees over there look like ponderosa pines, and I know I just saw an Abert's squirrel, but I think these trees are bristlecones—and isn't that an aspen grove? So what is this, the montane forest or the subalpine forest? I don't see any trees that look like Douglas-firs, and I sure don't see any lodgepole pines, so where the heck are we, anyway?

you're doing just what we'd hoped!

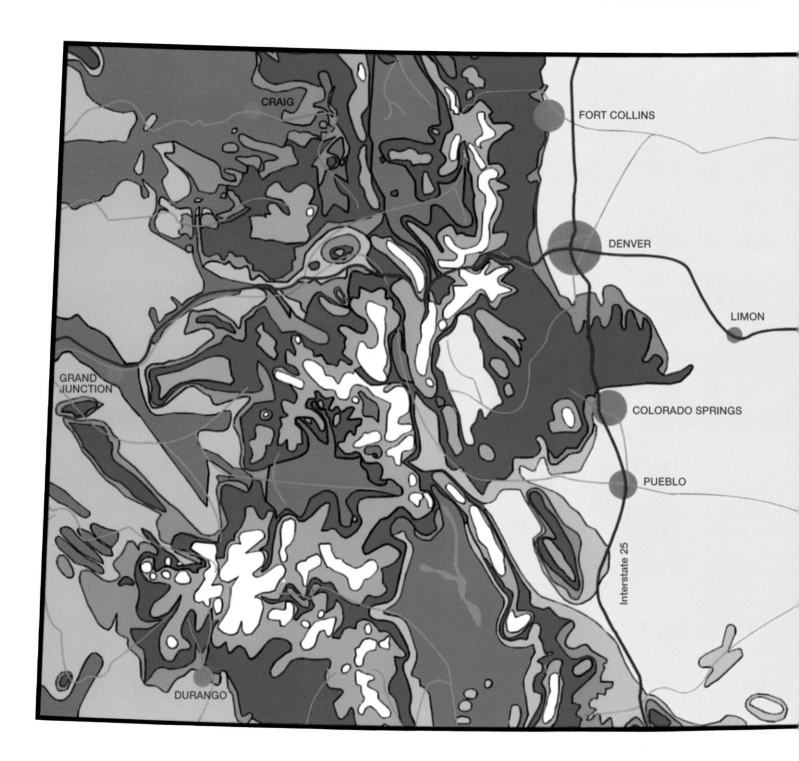

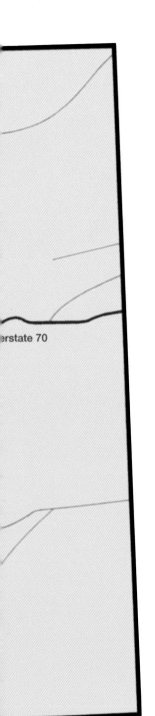

rstate 70

As always, nature simply is. The classifications we humans like to use to define it are subject to observation, discussion, debate, and argument—in short, to interpretation.

So which ecosystem DO you think you're in? Are several mixed together? Are you at the border between two different ecosystems? What are the clues? Which plant IS that? Have you seen any animals? If you're looking and wondering, you're following the naturalist's path.

This book is organized by ecosystem, from grassland to alpine tundra. Although treeline is not actually an ecosystem in its own right, it nonetheless has a section devoted to it. Each ecosystem section includes a description, called *Introducing the Ecosystem,* and a Denver Museum of Natural History diorama photograph. Scrapbook-style *Naturalist's Notes* follow, reminiscent of the seasonal observations and sketches a naturalist might record in the field. *Scenes and Seasons*, as seen through the camera lens, and *Illustrated Checklist* of plant and animal species, where you can make note of your own sightings, finish up each ecosystem section.

Grassland

Semidesert Shrubland

Piñon-Juniper Woodland

Riparian Land

Montane Shrubland

Montane Forest

Subalpine Forest

Treeline

Alpine Tundra

Now, let's Explore Colorado— from Plains to Peaks!

Grassland

often strip the grasslands of snow, building sculptured drifts. What snow is left melts quickly, or is carried off by warm chinook winds. The grasslands average only about 14 inches of moisture each year.

Prairie dog town

ou know you're in Colorado's grasslands when you see a prairie dog poking its head up from the ground or hear a horned lark's courtship song—with not a tree in sight.

Grasslands are too dry for trees to grow but too wet to be deserts. They cover flat or rolling land and have fine-textured, deep soils. Colorado's plains grasslands consist mostly of short grasses such as buffalograss and blue grama, with other low-growing, drought-resistant plants such as yucca, prickly pear cactus, and prairie coneflower growing among them.

Grasslands are hot, sunny, and dry in the summer. They are cold, windy, and dry in the winter. Most of the precipitation in Colorado's grasslands falls as spring showers or summer thunderstorms. Fierce winds

Colorado's grasslands are part of the Great Plains. Grasslands cover the eastern third of the state, usually at elevations below 5,500 feet. Sometimes, however, grasslands are found higher—in wide, flat mountain valleys. These high grasslands are called "parks," such as South Park or Middle Park, and have different species of plants.

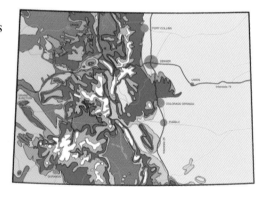

Grassland

Blue grama

Animals adapted to life in the grasslands have to cope with dryness, intense summer heat, and lack of trees. Although we usually associate birds with trees, many birds make their home in the grasslands. They've found other ways to make do— they sing while they're flying and build their nests on the ground.

Or animals can burrow beneath the earth. Many grassland animals live underground in burrows and "towns" dug into the grasslands' fine, dry soils.

Underground living arrangements also let animals escape the heat of the summer sun and keep up their moisture levels. Swift foxes, badgers, kangaroo rats, gophers, mice, voles— and of course prairie dogs—all dig and live in burrows. Prairie dog towns, in fact, often provide homes for other grassland animals such as burrowing owls, rattlesnakes, ferrets, and insects—in addition to the prairie dogs themselves.

(left) Plover and (right) burrowing owls

No trees means few places to hide. Grassland animals take advantage of what little cover there is— like ground-nesting birds and their eggs that are camouflaged among the grasses. Some can run away—like jackrabbits, which run fast to escape from coyotes and foxes. (The pronghorn, another swift grassland species, became a fast runner to escape an old enemy, the now-extinct North American cheetah.)

Swift fox

Although people often think of the flat eastern plains of Colorado as grassland, very little natural native grassland remains. Most of it has been developed, cultivated, or grazed. Pawnee Buttes in the Pawnee National Grassland, near Keota in northeastern Colorado, is a good place to go to see "unspoiled" grasslands—the way they used to be. Native animals, grasses, and other plants are encouraged. In early spring, the Pawnee National Grassland is a fabulous place for bird-watching!

As Far As the Eye Can See

Vast grasslands once swept hundreds of miles eastward from the Rocky Mountains. In this diorama, the prairie, dotted with the blooms of prickly pear and a multitude of prairie flowers, stretches beyond the jutting shapes of Pawnee Buttes to the distant horizon. On a late springtime afternoon, the treeless prairie teems with bird life—a mountain plover and its downy chick, lark buntings protecting their eggs, a horned lark, and a host of others. This scene is set within Pawnee National Grassland, near the Colorado–Wyoming border, one of very few areas where native grasses still grow wild.

Pawnee National Grassland

Notes & Observations in the Colorado grasslands, spring & summer

APRIL—The grasses are greening up! Once grasslands swept eastward for hundreds of miles. Pronghorn and bison roamed, hunted only by wolves and Indians.

Those days are gone . . . Few places even look like the early grasslands, let alone have native grasses.

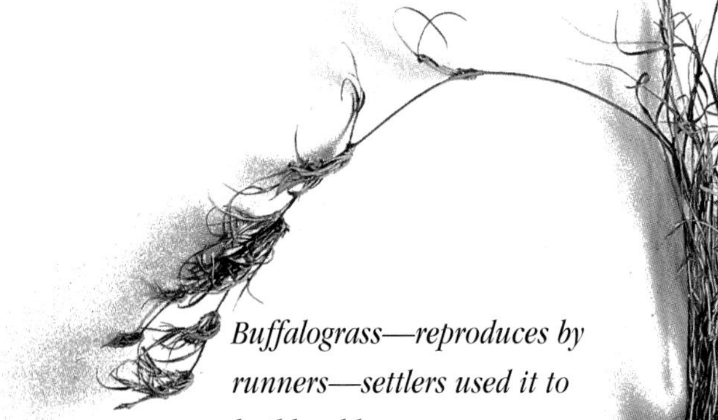

Buffalograss—reproduces by runners—settlers used it to build sod houses.
(Could be great for lawns in semi-arid climates—like Denver!)

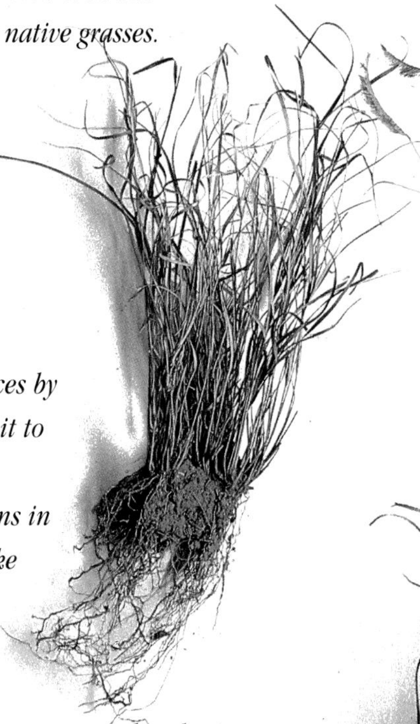

Blue grama—an abundant grass on the Colorado plains.

NOTE—Short-term, migratory grazing (bison, pronghorn) is beneficial to grasslands. Long-term, concentrated grazing (cattle, sheep) can kill plants and destroy grasslands.

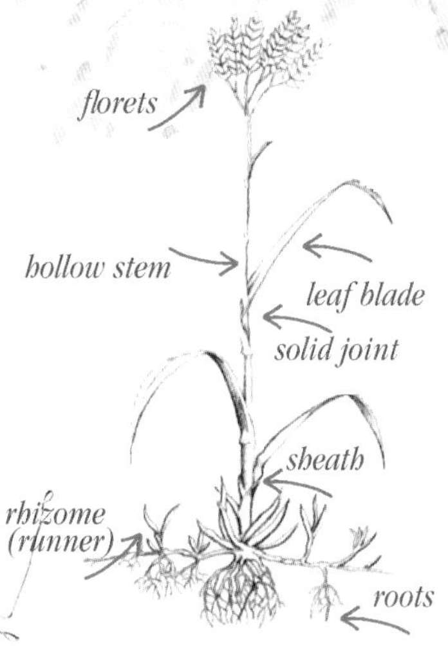

florets

hollow stem

leaf blade

solid joint

sheath

rhizome (runner)

roots

Grasses grow from the base, not from the tip the way trees do. Sugarcane, wheat, rye, barley, oats, corn, and rice are all grasses.

Prairie dogs have lived in Colorado for at least 450,000 years. They
- aerate & mix soil by digging burrows, reducing the "compacting" effect of hooves.
- provide ready-made homes for other animals.
- are a prime food source for hawks, eagles & other predators.

Once upon a time, black-footed ferrets had it made—eating prairie dogs AND living in their burrows. Hopefully they'll be reintroduced in Colorado (not a single native lives here now).

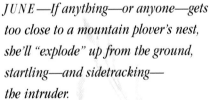

A Land Without Trees

MAY—Horned lark courtship is a sight to behold! A bird circles down from high in the sky, singing a tinkling, high-pitched flight song. When the song ends, he plummets, headfirst, wings closed until the last second.

- *BECAUSE THERE ARE NO TREES, many prairie bird species sing on the wing—after all, there's almost nowhere to perch.*

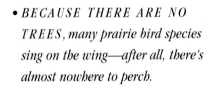

- *BECAUSE THERE ARE NO TREES, many prairie birds nest on the ground, where they need strategies for staying hidden and avoiding hooves—first bison and pronghorn, now cattle.*

JUNE—If anything—or anyone—gets too close to a mountain plover's nest, she'll "explode" up from the ground, startling—and sidetracking— the intruder.

Explore
COLORADO

The afternoon sun illuminates rolling hills of prairie sandreed and sand sagebrush in the sand hills of the South Platte River drainage.

A lark bunting, Colorado's state bird, takes a moment's rest on a bright pink musk thistle in the grasslands.

*Richly varied grassland plants, a portrait of what lies
on the mesas beyond, cover an eroded mesa top near
Castle Rock.*

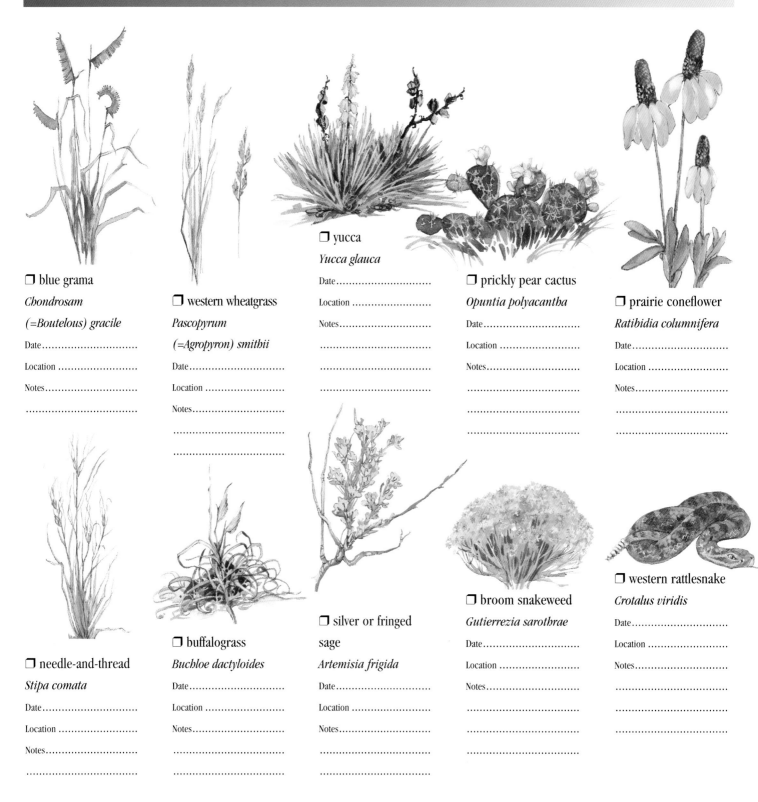

❏ blue grama

*Chondrosam
(=Boutelous) gracile*

Date.............................

Location ....

Notes............................

....

❏ needle-and-thread

Stipa comata

Date.............................

Location ....

Notes............................

....

❏ western wheatgrass

*Pascopyrum
(=Agropyron) smithii*

Date.............................

Location ....

Notes............................

....

....

❏ buffalograss

Buchloe dactyloides

Date.............................

Location ....

Notes............................

....

....

❏ yucca

Yucca glauca

Date.............................

Location ....

Notes............................

....

....

❏ silver or fringed
sage

Artemisia frigida

Date.............................

Location ....

Notes............................

....

....

❏ prickly pear cactus

Opuntia polyacantha

Date.............................

Location ....

Notes............................

....

....

❏ broom snakeweed

Gutierrezia sarothrae

Date.............................

Location ....

Notes............................

....

....

❏ prairie coneflower

Ratibidia columnifera

Date.............................

Location ....

Notes............................

....

....

❏ western rattlesnake

Crotalus viridis

Date.............................

Location ....

Notes............................

....

....

....

❐ **bullsnake**

Pituophis melanoleucus

Date............................

Location ....

Notes............................

....

....

....

❐ **western meadowlark**

Sturnella neglecta

Date............................

Location ....

Notes............................

....

....

❐ **lark bunting**

Colorado's state bird

Calamospiza melanocorys

Date............................

Location ....

Notes............................

....

....

❐ **pronghorn**

Antilocapra americana

Date............................

Location ....

Notes............................

....

❐ **black-tailed prairie dog**

Cynomys ludovicianus

Date............................

Location ....

Notes............................

....

❐ **horned lark**

Eremophila alpestris

Date............................

Location ....

Notes............................

....

....

....

❐ **golden eagle**

Aquila chrysaetos

Date............................

Location ....

Notes............................

....

....

....

❐ **red-tailed hawk**

Buteo jamaicensis

Date............................

Location ....

Notes............................

....

....

❐ **black-tailed jackrabbit**

Lepus californicus

Date............................

Location ....

Notes............................

....

❐ **thirteen-lined ground squirrel**

Spermophilus tridecemlineatus

Date............................

Location ....

Notes............................

....

....

When the white flanks of pronghorn flash at you from muted, gray-green vistas of rabbitbrush and sage, when you notice crusty, white patches of alkali on the bare ground or smell the warm, tangy odor of sun-warmed sage, then you know you're in the semidesert shrublands.

Pronghorn

Semidesert shrublands are Colorado's "cool deserts," hot as blazes in the summer but with winter temperatures well below zero degrees Fahrenheit. They are dominated by greasewood, saltbush, sagebrush, rabbitbrush, and other shrubs that grow long taproots to capture moisture from deep within the soil. Semidesert shrublands are some of the most distinctive sights in western and southern Colorado. Most of the precipitation in this ecosystem falls as snow, with moisture averaging less than 10 inches per year.

Semidesert shrublands in Colorado form the eastern edge of the Great Basin and Colorado Plateau. They cover a broad range of elevations—from 5,000 to over 10,000 feet. In western Colorado, they follow canyons and rivers into mountain valleys and onto high plateaus. Semidesert shrublands also are found in the San Luis Valley, North Park, Middle Park, and the Gunnison Basin.

Semidesert shrubland

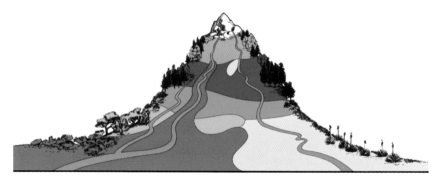

Greasewood is toxic—or at least unpleasant—to many animals because of the soil it grows in, but it is good food for species adapted to it, such as black-tailed jackrabbits. Sagebrush voles feed on greasewood, too, along with sagebrush and other shrubs. Mule deer and pronghorn find both sagebrush and bitterbrush just fine for browsing. Fleet-footed pronghorn love the short vegetation and wide-open spaces.

Greasewood

For some animals, semidesert shrublands are truly home. These animals have adapted to dryness, alkaline soils, winter cold, and summer heat. Many small semidesert mammals don't need to drink water at all! Ord's kangaroo rats, for example, get all the water they need from the plants they eat.

Many birds hide among the shrubs to protect themselves from heat and cold. Their names give you a clue to their preferred habitat: sage sparrows, sage thrashers, and especially sage grouse. These birds are found only in the West's wide, rolling semidesert shrublands.

Ord's kangaroo rat

Black-tailed jackrabbit

Blooming rabbitbrush and sunflowers in the San Luis Valley

Many people find semidesert shrublands empty and desolate. But for those who love the West, they conjure up images of earlier times and nature's timeless rhythms. Inhospitable as they may seem, semidesert shrublands remain less touched by the relentless crawl of development than other ecosystems.

One of the best places to get out of your car and experience the subtle life of this ecosystem is just off State Highway 13 north of Craig. Go in March or April. Scout the area beforehand to find an open area, then return before dawn—you may see the sage grouse dance! The pronghorn viewing area along State Highway 22 northeast of Kremmling is another good place to stop and smell the sage.

Sage-Covered Hills

Broad vistas of purple-tinged sage stretch for miles across the land, as a May dawn breaks over the rolling hills near northwest Colorado's Elkhead Mountains. The morning light in this diorama scene highlights the surprise of yellow balsam-root and the vibrant blue of chiming bells—and reveals a drama of high-desert courtship. Females watch a select of male sage grouse—white-chested, with tails spread like fans—shiver, shake, boom, and strut from dawn until after sunup. This annual spring ritual determines future generations, as females select their mates from among the performers.

Southeast of the Elkhead Mountains

Notes & Observations in the sagebrush shrublands, winter & spring

DECEMBER—Snow brings much-needed moisture to this shrubby, rolling land.

Sagebrush has small leaves that stay on all winter. In spring, larger leaves develop—only to drop off again in summer when the soil dries out.

Rabbitbrush is often found with sagebrush.

With their deep roots, these shrubs can survive on just winter moisture, so they thrive in western Colorado. Grasses, on the other hand, have shallow roots and need summer moisture, so they thrive in eastern Colorado.

Spectacular Courtship

FEBRUARY—In late winter, male sage grouse begin to leave their winter quarters, headed for their strutting grounds—open areas called leks—among the sage.

February 27

MARCH 5—At the lek, males face off— each takes his turn to compete for position. They keep this up for weeks till the pecking order is sorted out . . .

APRIL 1—Once the hens arrive, they get to watch daily displays of booming, strutting, puffing, and popping that last from dawn to 8 A.M. or so. Eventually the hens choose mates from among the performers. Once, as many as 400 male sage grouse gathered at a single lekking ground. Now a dozen or so is a good show . . . (Once again, habitat loss is taking its toll.)

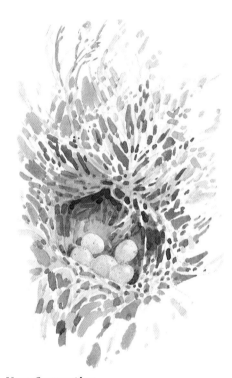

New Generation

APRIL 12—A week after breeding, hens scratch out shallow nests between plants and line them with grass, twigs, and feathers. (Grouse hatching is timed to coincide with a ready supply of water and insects in the shrublands.)

Backlit by the morning sun, a male pronghorn feeds on the growth of early summer in the San Luis Valley.

(below) A light snow sticks to shrubs and rocks, but not the ground, highlighting the layers of Unaweep Canyon near Gateway in western Colorado.

*The sculpted dunes
of Great Sand Dunes
National Monument rise
from a sea of
rabbitbrush,
punctuated by the
yellow of cottonwoods
in early fall.*

❒ greasewood

Sarcobatus vermiculatus

Date.............................

Location ....

Notes............................

....

....

❒ big sagebrush

Seriphidium
tridentatum

Date.............................

Location ....

Notes............................

....

....

....

❒ paintbrush

Castilleja sp.

Date.............................

Location ....

Notes............................

....

....

....

❒ galleta grass

Hilaria jamesii

Date.............................

Location ....

Notes............................

....

❒ eastern fence lizard

Sceloporus undulatus

Date.............................

Location ....

Notes............................

....

....

❒ rabbitbrush

Chrysothamnus spp.

Date.............................

Location ....

Notes............................

....

....

....

❒ four-winged
saltbush

Atriplex canescens

Date.............................

Location ....

Notes............................

....

....

❒ arrowleaf balsam-
root

Balsamorhiza sagittata

Date.............................

Location ....

Notes............................

....

❒ squirrel tail

Elymus (=Sitanion)
hystrix

Date.............................

Location ....

Notes............................

❒ sagebrush lizard

Sceloporus graciosus

Date.............................

Location ....

Notes............................

....

....

....

❏ western rattlesnake

Crotalus viridis

Date.............................

Location ....

Notes.............................

....

....

....

❏ sage thrasher

Oreoscoptes montanus

Date.............................

Location ....

Notes.............................

....

❏ canyon towhee

Pipilo fuscus

Date.............................

Location ....

Notes.............................

....

....

❏ desert cottontail

Sylvilagus audubonii

Date.............................

Location ....

Notes.............................

....

....

❏ black-tailed jackrabbit

Lepus californicus

Date.............................

Location ....

Notes.............................

....

....

❏ Ord's kangaroo rat

Dipodomys ordii

Date.............................

Location ....

Notes.............................

....

....

❏ sage grouse

Centrocercus urophasianus

Date.............................

Location ....

Notes.............................

....

....

❏ golden eagle

Aquila chrysaetos

Date.............................

Location ....

Notes.............................

....

....

❏ Brewer's sparrow

Spizella breweri

Date.............................

Location ....

Notes.............................

....

....

....

❏ coyote

Canis latrans

Date.............................

Location ....

Notes.............................

....

....

....

Piñon pine cones

Piñon-juniper woodland

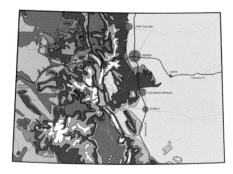

Y ou're probably in the pygmy forest—another name for piñon-juniper woodlands—when you see short evergreens, evenly and widely spaced on hillsides, with not much growing between them. If you can identify the trees as piñon pines and junipers, you know for sure. The trunks of junipers are often gnarled and twisted, and piñons rarely grow taller then 30 feet.

Piñon pines and juniper trees grow together where few other trees can survive—in coarse, gravelly soil in warm, dry areas. They get only between 10 and 20 inches of precipitation each year, but coarse soils let the water soak deep enough to support trees. Piñons are more cold-tolerant and tend to grow at higher elevations; drought-tolerant junipers dominate the lower slopes.

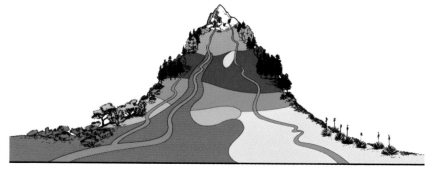

Piñon-juniper woodlands are among Colorado's lowest evergreen forests and sometimes form a transition between grasslands or shrublands below and montane forests—if there are any—above. The woodlands grow along mesa slopes, hills, mountain flanks, and ridges in western and southern Colorado. On the eastern slope, they're usually found south of Colorado Springs—but there is one lone stand at Owl Canyon, north of Fort Collins!

Bighorn sheep

Piñon-juniper woodlands look awfully dry, but they are filled with animals that thrive in this warm, open ecosystem. Elk, mule deer, pronghorn, and even bighorn sheep browse the woodlands in winter and spring.

Brushy areas provide cover year-round and the trees provide food for piñon mice and woodrats. In the fall when the juniper berries and piñon nuts are ripe, many animals migrate to the woodlands to share the feast. Even black bears sometimes show up!

Woodland birds play a big role in helping the trees disperse their seeds. The distinctive piñon jay's special relationship with piñon pines gives it its name. Tree feeds bird, bird plants tree!

Piñon jay and piñon mouse

Piñon pines below La Garita Arch

Piñon-juniper woodlands are unique and interesting places, with a long history of human use, ranging from gathering piñon nuts to cutting down trees for building material and grazing cattle. Unfortunately, the trees grow slowly and overgrazed woodlands are very slow to recover. Today, one of the best places to find them—and even look for piñon nuts—is the La Garita–Penitente Canyon area on the west side of the San Luis Valley in southern Colorado. In western Colorado, Colorado National Monument near Grand Junction is a good place to explore the pygmy forest.

The Pygmy Forest

A gnarled juniper tree and nearby piñon pines shelter birds, reptiles, and insects in this diorama scene, set near Mesa Verde in southwestern Colorado. Piñons and junipers nearly always grow together, alongside shorter dry-country plants like blooming prickly pear, claret cup, and other cactus plants. Well-hidden birds in this late-spring scene include brown towhees, blue-gray gnatcatchers, grayish-colored bushtits, and mottled scaled quail—in addition to the ever-present piñon jays. The quail family—a male, female, and clutch of tiny babies—nests among lichen-covered rocks that also conceal several lizards and a tarantula.

Mesa Verde National Park

Notes & Observations in a piñon-juniper woodland, fall & winter

NOTE—Almost every animal that lives here eats piñon nuts or juniper berries—or eats some other animal that eats piñon nuts or juniper berries . . . (The trees are primary producers.)

No other Colorado trees can get by on so little water, so piñon pines and junipers are the only trees in these woodlands. The less water they get, the slower they grow and the more gnarled they look—but they survive!

Needles and scales are kinds of leaves. Their waxy surfaces conserve moisture.

Juniper berries are modified cones (and they're used to make gin—sniff one sometime!).

DECEMBER—When it's really cold in the high country, mule deer come down from the hills. They'd rather eat plant leaves and twigs but make do with browsing on juniper, rabbitbrush, and even piñon needles.

Tree feeds bird,
bird plants tree

SEPTEMBER—The piñon nuts are ripe! Piñon jays are everywhere, pecking cones open to get at the nuts. They stockpile lots of nuts for winter.

Jays do piñon trees a real service by "planting" their nuts below the surface in moist soil. If the seeds lie on top of the ground, the afternoon sun heats them up and they dry out . . .
(Some of the forgotten seeds will become trees.)

Piñon nuts=piñon tree seeds.

People eat piñon nuts, too. They taste like fat, juicy sunflower seeds.

OCTOBER—A piñon mouse lives in a hollow juniper branch nearby. It scurries around the area eating juniper seeds—and insects and nuts.

Many other animals use piñon-juniper woodlands as a seasonal home. Jackrabbits find food here during heavy snow.

October 13, 7:15 P.M.

Ringtails are hunters, shy and elusive—but friendly enough that lonely miners sometimes kept them as pets. (They're related to raccoons.)

There are lots of rodents in P-J country: rock squirrels, Colorado chipmunks, Mexican woodrats, deer mice.

Along with the local quail, all these rodents give ringtails and other predators plenty to eat.

Like a fluid work of abstract art, the lines and colors of this twisted piñon pine bear witness to its long life.

A knobby green blanket of piñon-juniper woodland covers these slopes at the edge of the Colorado Plateau in the Four Corners area.

As if staking out their territory, piñon pines and a few junipers space themselves evenly across these dry, southwestern Colorado hills.

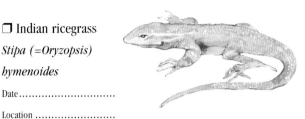

❒ **Indian ricegrass**
Stipa (=Oryzopsis)
hymenoides

Date............................

Location ....

Notes...........................

....

....

....

❒ piñon pine

Pinus edulis

Date............................

Location ....

Notes...........................

....

....

....

❒ **one-seed juniper**

Sabina (=Juniperus)
monosperma

Date............................

Location ....

Notes...........................

....

....

....

....

❒ **bitterbrush**

Purshia tridentata

Date............................

Location ....

Notes...........................

....

....

....

❒ side-blotched lizard

Uta stansburiana

Date............................

Location ....

Notes...........................

....

....

....

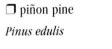

❒ **Utah juniper**

Sabina (=Juniperus)
osteosperma

Date............................

Location ....

Notes...........................

....

....

❒ **mountain-mahogany**

Cercocarpus montanus

Date............................

Location ....

Notes...........................

....

....

....

❒ Junegrass

Koelaria macrantha

Date............................

Location ....

Notes...........................

....

....

❒ **collared lizard**

Crotaphytus collaris

Date............................

Location ....

Notes...........................

....

....

❒ piñon jay

Gymnorhinus
cyanocephalus

Date............................

Location ....

Notes...........................

....

....

❑ **plain titmouse**

Parus inornatus

Date.............................

Location ....

Notes...........................

....

....

❑ **common poorwill**

Phalaenoptilus nuttallii

Date.............................

Location ....

Notes...........................

....

....

....

❑ **blue-gray gnatcatcher**

Polioptila caerulea

Date.............................

Location ....

Notes...........................

....

....

....

❑ **mountain cottontail**

Sylvilagus nuttallii

Date.............................

Location ....

Notes...........................

....

....

❑ **mountain lion**

Felis concolor

Date.............................

Location ....

Notes...........................

....

....

❑ **bushtit**

Psaltriparus minimus

Date.............................

Location ....

Notes...........................

....

....

....

❑ **American kestrel**

Falco sparverius

Date.............................

Location ....

Notes...........................

....

....

❑ **piñon mouse**

Peromyscus truei

Date.............................

Location ....

Notes...........................

....

....

....

❑ **pallid bat**

Antrozous pallidus

Date.............................

Location ....

Notes...........................

....

....

❑ **ringtail**

Bassariscus astutus

Date.............................

Location ....

Notes...........................

....

....

....

Riparian Land

Willow

f there's water, you're in a riparian area! Whether a lake or stream high in the mountains, or a pond or river in the lowlands, riparian areas are unmistakeable—as much for their lush vegetation and many animal residents as for the water itself. In Colorado, willows and cottonwoods are particularly good hints that water is nearby.

Riparian lands include the edges of streams, rivers, ponds, lakes, and marshes. They offer good cover, plenty of water, and abundant food. Because riparian areas occur in many different locations, temperatures and precipitation vary widely. But all riparian areas have more available moisture than the surrounding countryside.

Riparian lands are found within all other Colorado ecosystems, and they occur at all elevations. Up high, they include sedges, blue spruce trees, and white firs, along with the ever-present willows. At lower elevations, cottonwoods, box-elders, and willows grow along the water's edge. Cattails and bulrushes are found in marshy areas around ponds.

Western tanager

Riparian land

Many animals that are usually found in Colorado's other ecosystems visit riparian areas from time to time. After all, there's water to drink and lush foliage to eat! Predators, such as weasels and foxes, are attracted by the promise of prey. Migrating birds use riparian lands as resting places in the spring and fall, and many nest in them as well.

But some animals can live only in riparian habitats. Beavers, for instance, are great swimmers and depend on water and the trees that grow nearby to make their lodges—and for food, too! Red-winged blackbirds perch and nest among the cattails in marshy areas. Ducks, herons, and other waterfowl eat fish and other foods found only in water. Dippers are especially charming riparian birds, dashing about and dipping into mountain streams. Amphibians—several frogs, salamanders, great plains toads, and, higher up, the extremely rare boreal toad—are dependent on watery habitats for

Late fall at Barr Lake

Great blue heron

Although Colorado is generally a dry state, there are plenty of good places to see riparian lands. Barr Lake is a lowland lake, just off Interstate 76 northeast of Denver, with handicapped access trails and a visitor center. The South Platte River greenway, stretching from Chatfield Reservoir north into Denver, is a great place to stroll and get close to wildlife. Hanging Lake, off Interstate 70 east of Glenwood Springs, is a lovely mountain lake reached by a short, but steep, trail. For a special treat, visit the fully accessible Sugarloaf Campground Boardwalk at the Williams Fork River, off State Highway 3 south of Parshall. A network of boardwalks crisscrosses the river, passing through alders and willows. You can even watch beavers at work from decks and seating areas.

laying their eggs. Dragonflies, water-dwellers during their larval stage, are a common sight around Colorado's waterways.

Many riparian species are strictly aquatic. Fish, for instance, breathe oxygen from the water through gills, instead of lungs like land-dwelling animals. Trout, which need a lot of oxygen, frequent the cold, oxygen-rich waters of mountain streams.

Tree-Top Sanctuary

High cottonwoods are a lush, leafy home for great blue herons, snowy egrets, and black-crowned night herons. Wings spread, a great blue heron is poised to fly to the river—where it will fish and bring back food for the hungry month-old chicks in the nest. Such timeless scenes are common along Colorado's waterways and lake edges. This diorama portrays a view of the South Platte River— with Mount Evans in the distance—in an area that is now submerged, covered by the waters of Chatfield Reservoir. The birds are still a familiar sight but now nest in rookeries along the lakeshore.

South Platte River

Notes & Observations in a riparian ecosystem, summer

Wetlands now cover only about 3% of Colorado, but they contain most of the state's wildlife.

Muskrat swimming

Spiny soft-shelled turtle

Cottonwood trees are like "footprints" of the river. Trees far from the water sometimes mark channels abandoned long ago.

Layers of Life

How can so many animals live in one place? Layering—sort of like a high-rise apartment in the city—is part of the answer.

tree canopy

underbrush

surface

underwater

underground

Finding a Niche

In this rookery (communal nesting area where the heron families live), each kind of heron clearly has its own niche. Using the same river and tree
- they nest at different levels in the tree.
- some feed in shallow water, some in deep.
- some feed in the day, others at night.

JUNE 3 • Mid-morning

Head raised, neck folded, this great blue heron flew to the river from its nest in the top of a tree. Motionless in 15 inches of water, all but invisible, it watches for a fish, frog, or salamander.

SPLASH—A fish appears in the heron's beak.

• Late morning

Snowy egrets joined the great blue at the river. Darting about in the shallows, they stir up the water and stab for fish or insects. The egrets carry fish back to their youngsters (waiting—not so patiently—in the tree canopy).

• Twilight

A black-crowned night heron left its nest—lower in the cottonwood—crying a harsh "gwok!" Large, stocky, with short legs (for a heron, that is), it stands, hunched, in the edge waters, looking for fish or small reptiles. When the bird gets a fish, it shakes it—hard—to stun it.

Snow and the misty cold of winter subdue the already fading yellow of aspens along the White River, not far from the town of Meeker.

(left) Spring-green cottonwoods, cattails, and grasses in this watery oasis grace the rocky grandeur of Dominguez Canyon in the Uncompahgre Plateau.

(right) Morning reveals tracks along a sandy riverbank in the San Luis Valley, clues to a late summer night's comings and goings.

*A mountain stream rushes down a rocky course,
cutting through a field of pink Parry's primrose and
other flowers high in the Mount Zirkel Wilderness
near Walden.*

❒ bulrush

Schoenoplectus
(=Scirpus) lacustris

Date..............................

Location ....

Notes.............................

....

....

❒ sedges

Carex spp.

Date..............................

Location ....

Notes.............................

....

....

❒ cow parsnip

Heracleum sphondylium

Date..............................

Location ....

Notes.............................

....

....

❒ willow

Salix spp.

Date..............................

Location ....

Notes.............................

....

....

❒ Woodhouse's toad

Bufo woodhousii

Date..............................

Location ....

Notes.............................

....

....

....

....

❒ broad-leaved cattail

Typha latifolia

Date..............................

Location ....

Notes.............................

....

....

....

❒ bittercress

Cardamine cordifolia

Date..............................

Location ....

Notes.............................

....

❒ box-elder

Negundo (=Acer)
aceroides

Date..............................

Location ....

Notes.............................

....

❒ tiger salamander

Ambystoma tigrinum

Date..............................

Location ....

Notes.............................

....

....

❒ striped
chorus frog

Pseudacris
triseriata

Date..............................

Location ....

Notes.............................

....

....

....

❒ western terrestrial garter snake

Thamnophis elegans

Date.............................

Location ....

Notes...........................

....

❒ plains garter snake

Thamnophis radix

Date.............................

Location ....

Notes...........................

....

❒ American dipper

Cinclus mexicanus

Date.............................

Location ....

Notes...........................

....

❒ belted kingfisher

Ceryle alcyon

Date.............................

Location ....

Notes...........................

....

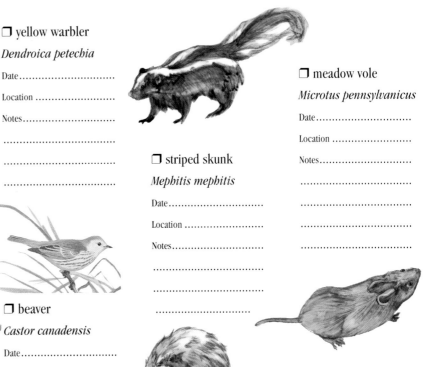

❒ great horned owl

Bube virginianus

Date.............................

Location ....

Notes...........................

....

....

....

❒ great blue heron

Ardea herodias

Date.............................

Location ....

Notes...........................

....

....

❒ yellow warbler

Dendroica petechia

Date.............................

Location ....

Notes...........................

....

....

....

....

❒ beaver

Castor canadensis

Date.............................

Location ....

Notes...........................

....

....

....

❒ striped skunk

Mephitis mephitis

Date.............................

Location ....

Notes...........................

....

....

....

❒ muskrat

Ondatra zibethicus

Date.............................

Location ....

Notes...........................

....

....

....

❒ meadow vole

Microtus pennsylvanicus

Date.............................

Location ....

Notes...........................

....

....

....

❒ white-tailed deer

Odocoileus hemionus

Date.............................

Location ....

Notes...........................

....

....

Scrub oak

Montane shrublands are found along the lower elevations of Colorado's mountains and foothills, below the montane forest. They form a patchy, narrow belt along the eastern foothills. On the western slope of the mountains, montane shrublands cover larger areas.

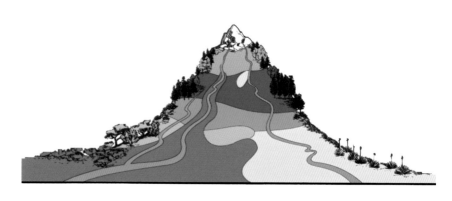

Scraggly thickets of scrub oak growing in dry, rocky places are a sure sign that you're in montane shrubland. In the fall, montane shrublands turn orange and red—some of the best fall color to be found in Colorado.

Sumac, serviceberry, mountain-mahogany, and the easily recognized lobe-leaved scrub oak are some of the shrubs that grow in the coarse soils on the rocky terrain of the montane shrublands. Usually not enough moisture falls in montane shrublands— they don't get much more precipitation than grasslands—for full-size trees to grow (although when scrub oaks find ideal conditions in which to grow, they can get pretty big).

Montane shrubland

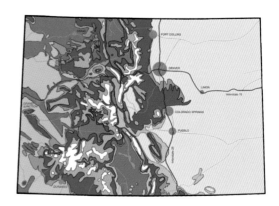

It's especially easy to find montane shrublands in the fall—just look for the red leaves! Montane shrublands occur in various places all along the foothills west of Denver and Colorado Springs. Red Rocks Park, near Morrison, is a spectacular setting to explore the shrublands. Bear Creek Canyon Regional Park, near Manitou Springs, has a nature center as well as self-guided nature trails along thickets of scrub oak.

Mountain-mahogany, a somewhat ragged-looking shrub, has wonderful, self-planting seeds. The long, curved, fuzzy "tail" allows the seed to float downward, seed first. Then the tail twists up, driving the seed into the ground like a drill bit. Montane shrublands produce abundant seeds, fruits, and nuts—making them a busy place during the fall harvest. Mice, spotted skunks, foxes, coyotes, black bears, and lots of birds fill themselves on the shrubland's bounty.

Mountain-mahogany

Shrublands provide good nesting and denning sites for mammals. Chipmunks, ground squirrels, deer mice, bobcats, and even mountain lions are common. You'll often see bright orange lichen on the rocks where many small mammals live—it thrives in nitrogen-rich areas where urine collects outside animal dens.

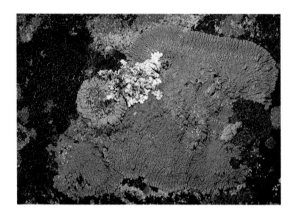

Orange lichen

Flocks of birds, especially noisy bands of scrub jays, inhabit the shrublands. Rufous-sided towhees, indigo buntings, and Virginia's warblers sing from the dense branches where they build well-protected nests. Scaled quail find both food and shelter in the montane shrublands.

A golden-mantled ground squirrel feeds on flowers.

Land of Plenty

Surrounded by a mosaic of color—the bright blue of asters and the contrasting array of red-golds among the sumac, skunkbrush, and scrub oak—plants and animals of Colorado's foothills prepare for winter. Here at the entrance to Jarre Canyon, in the foothills between Denver and Colorado Springs, sharp-tailed grouse wander among the vividly colored montane shrublands in this early October diorama scene. Band-tailed pigeons perch in the branches of an oak on the right, while a scrub jay scolds from a higher oak branch on the left. Shrublands offer shelter and food to a great diversity of life, especially during the autumn harvest of acorns and berries.

Jarre Canyon

Notes & Observations in the montane shrublands, fall & spring

O C T O B E R — "Hogback" is a good description of the rocky ridges along the foothills— they look like a razorback hog's bristly back . . .

When the Rockies were formed, layers of sedimentary rock were pushed up along the eastern edge of the mountains. Soft rock layers have long since eroded away, leaving the harder ridges exposed.

Why Leaves Change Color:

❶ *As winter approaches, days get shorter, temperatures drop, and sunlight weakens. Leaves stop producing chlorophyll (which is—among other things—a green pigment).*

❷ *At the same time, existing chlorophyll begins to break down.*

❸ *Orange and yellow pigments (which were there all along but were hidden by the chlorophyll) begin to show through.*

Getting Ready

OCTOBER 15—Autumn is a wonderful time of year. So much energy! Everything—plant and animal alike—is getting ready for the long winter months ahead.

OCTOBER 20—There must be a "pocket" of moisture here, to support such tall scrub oaks! Every part of the oak feeds some kind of animal:
- *Mule deer browse on twigs & branches.*
  - *Bandtailed pigeons, rock squirrels, and scrub jays eat acorns.*
- *Insects and larvae live under the bark and inside acorns.*

Ladies' Choice

OCTOBER 23—Some sharp-tailed grouse hens are foraging nearby—they eat grasshoppers, crickets, beetles, rose hips, berries, corn, wheat, and grains.

APRIL—Sharp-tailed grouse are doing their synchronized spring dance, and the females are watching . . .

Males raise their tails, droop their wings, and stretch out their necks. RAT-TAT-TAT! They rattle their tail feathers and stamp their feet. Around they go, pivoting unbelievably fast in semicircles. Females choose mates from among the dancers.

Bare trunks form a stately scrub oak promenade,
casting shadows on the snow-covered ground below
the Spanish Peaks in the San Isabel National Forest.

Scrub oaks are silhouetted like stained glass against the sky, grown tall in this moist thicket near Castle Rock.

Awash in the colors of fall, shrubs mingle with ponderosa pines on this Castle Rock hillside.

☐ needle-and-thread

Stipa comata

Date.............................

Location ....

Notes...........................

....

....

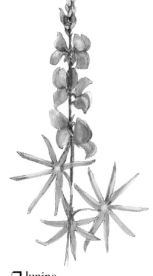

☐ **scrub oak**

Quercus gambelii

Date.............................

Location ....

Notes...........................

....

....

....

☐ **serviceberry**

Amelanchier spp.

Date.............................

Location ....

Notes...........................

....

....

....

☐ **smooth sumac**

Rhus glabra

Date.............................

Location ....

Notes...........................

....

....

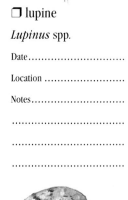

☐ **lupine**

Lupinus spp.

Date.............................

Location ....

Notes...........................

....

....

....

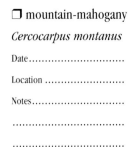

☐ **scarlet gilia**

Ipomopsis aggregata

Date.............................

Location ....

Notes...........................

....

....

....

☐ **mountain-mahogany**

Cercocarpus montanus

Date.............................

Location ....

Notes...........................

....

....

....

☐ **skunkbrush**

Rhus aromatica

Date.............................

Location ....

Notes...........................

....

....

....

☐ **snowberry**

Symphoricarpos spp.

Date.............................

Location ....

Notes...........................

....

....

....

☐ **bullsnake**

Pituophis melanoleucus

Date.............................

Location ....

Notes...........................

....

....

....

❐ scrub jay

Aphelocoma
coerulescens

Date.............................

Location ....

Notes.............................

....

....

❐ lazuli bunting

Passerina amoena

Date.............................

Location ....

Notes.............................

....

....

❐ Virginia's warbler

Vermivora virginiae

Date.............................

Location ....

Notes.............................

....

❐ wild turkey

Meleagris gallopavo

Date.............................

Location ....

Notes.............................

....

....

....

....

❐ green-tailed towhee

Pipilo chlorurus

Date.............................

Location ....

Notes.............................

....

....

....

❐ rufous-sided towhee

Pipilo erythrophthalmus

Date.............................

Location ....

Notes.............................

....

....

....

❐ deer mouse

Peromyscus
maniculatus

Date.............................

Location ....

Notes.............................

....

....

....

❐ gray fox

Urocyon
cinereoargenteus

Date.............................

Location ....

Notes.............................

....

....

....

❐ western spotted
skunk

Spilogale gracilis

Date.............................

Location ....

Notes.............................

....

....

....

❐ mule deer

Odocoileus hemionus

Date.............................

Location ....

Notes.............................

....

....

❐ rock squirrel

Spermophilus variegatus

Date.............................

Location ....

Notes.............................

....

....

❐ coyote

Canis latrans

Date.............................

Location ....

Notes.............................

....

....

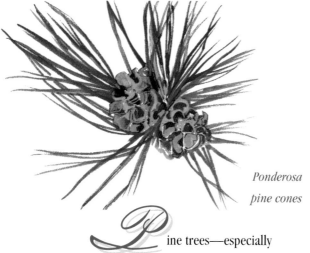

Ponderosa pine cones

Lots of grasses, shrubs, and wildflowers usually grow among montane forest trees. Annual precipitation in the montane is around 25 inches or less, with a lot of it falling as snow that melts within a few days. Summers are long, hot, and fairly dry.

Montane forests grow in a broad band along Colorado's mountainsides, below the dense subalpine forests and above the shrubby vegetation of lower elevations. They range in elevation from about 5,500 to 9,000 feet. Interestingly, the Black Forest northeast of Colorado Springs is a montane forest ecosystem—even though it isn't in the mountains!

ine trees—especially ponderosa pines—are a classic indicator that you're in the montane forest. Ponderosas are easy to recognize. They grow mostly on lower and south-facing slopes, and no other native Colorado conifer has such long needles. The needles are four to seven inches long and grow in bundles of two or three. Dense stands of Douglas-firs growing on cooler, wetter, north-facing slopes are another sure sign of the montane forest. Douglas-firs look very different from ponderosas—Douglas-fir trees are dark green and full, with flat, short needles.

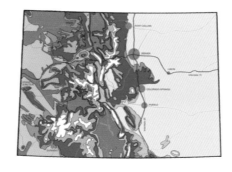

Montane forest

You often find aspen groves in the montane forest as well. Lodgepole pines, which are unmistakable, are found there, too. They look like fields of evenly spaced telephone poles, with not much in between them except fallen needles. Aspens, lodgepole pines, and Douglas-firs also grow higher up the mountains in subalpine forests.

Douglas-fir cone

Many animals live in montane forest ecosystems; a wide variety of food supports a wide variety of animal life. Birds, especially, are abundant. Some of them—like American crows, black-billed magpies, and Steller's jays—migrate down to the foothills and plains each day and return at night. Others—dark-eyed juncos, pine siskins, and wild turkeys—stay in the forest. Several reptiles like the montane forest, too, especially bullsnakes—which sometimes climb trees!

Steller's jay

Montane forests are found throughout the mountains. Many people have chosen to build their homes in the montane forest and more are being built every day. Some good places to experience undeveloped areas of Colorado's most familiar mountain ecosystem are White Ranch State Park west of Golden and Lookout Mountain Nature Center in Jefferson County Open Space, off Interstate 70 west of Denver. The Florissant Fossil Beds area in the Rampart Range, off State Highway 24 west of Colorado Springs, is also classic montane forest country.

Some animals, such as pygmy nuthatches, flammulated owls, mule deer, porcupines, and chipmunks, are almost synonymous with the montane forest. Abert's squirrels, with their big, distinctive, tasseled ears, are inseparable companions of ponderosa pines. The squirrels depend exclusively on ponderosas for food, nesting, and cover—and even have personal favorites among the trees. They love the ones that taste "just right" and sometimes strip them almost bare!

Abert's squirrel

Deer of the West

Alert to any approaching danger—with sensitive ears swiveled to pick up sounds—a young buck mule deer, a doe, and two yearlings browse among winter-bare aspen trunks and dry grasses. A Steller's jay watches from the branches of a young aspen. Evergreens cover the mountainsides beyond in this montane forest diorama, set near Pikes Peak west of Colorado Springs. Open areas to feed in and woods for shelter make for favored mule deer habitat. But winter grasses and shrubs are dry and low in nutrients, and with another storm approaching, the deer may soon move lower down the mountain.

Rampart Range

Notes & Observations in the montane forest, winter

Marvelous Mule Deer

Why are they called mule deer? Because of their big ears! Each ear turns independently to help mule deer hear far-away sounds.

March 6

Male mule deer shed their antlers every year. Countless little rodents gnaw on the "lost" antlers to add mineral nutrients to their diet.

Female Douglas-fir cones are large, with a spiky, three-tongued bract. Male Douglas-fir cones are small and orange-red.

The Trees ARE the Forest

Ponderosas and Douglas-firs are THE trees of the montane; ponderosas on south-facing slopes and dense stands of Douglas-firs on moist north slopes.

Did you know that ponderosa bark smells like vanilla? Try it yourself!

Ponderosa bark

Ponderosa reproduction is a dubious proposition . . . First of all, they don't reproduce until they're 25 years old. There's a heavy seed crop every 3 to 5 years, but it has to happen at the same time as an unusually wet spring for any seedlings to sprout.

Ponderosa pines have long needles, in bundles of 2 or 3.

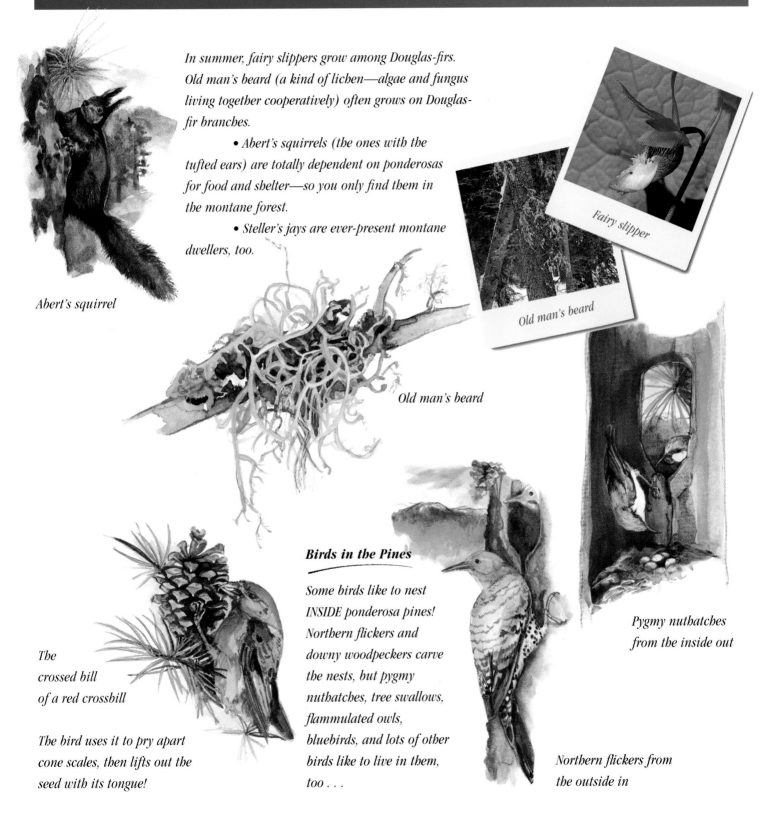

In summer, fairy slippers grow among Douglas-firs. Old man's beard (a kind of lichen—algae and fungus living together cooperatively) often grows on Douglas-fir branches.

• Abert's squirrels (the ones with the tufted ears) are totally dependent on ponderosas for food and shelter—so you only find them in the montane forest.

• Steller's jays are ever-present montane dwellers, too.

Abert's squirrel

Fairy slipper

Old man's beard

Old man's beard

Birds in the Pines

Some birds like to nest INSIDE ponderosa pines! Northern flickers and downy woodpeckers carve the nests, but pygmy nuthatches, tree swallows, flammulated owls, bluebirds, and lots of other birds like to live in them, too . . .

The crossed bill of a red crossbill

The bird uses it to pry apart cone scales, then lifts out the seed with its tongue!

Pygmy nuthatches from the inside out

Northern flickers from the outside in

Rich purple lupines carpet the forest floor beneath the arrow-straight trunks of lodgepole pines in the Sawatch Range.

Peering from a prickly circle of quills, a porcupine takes a break from feeding.

With winter food in short supply, a mule deer buck stretches for a ponderosa pine snack.

❒ ponderosa pine

Pinus ponderosa

Date..................................

Location............................

Notes................................

....

....

....

❒ Douglas-fir

Pseudotsuga menziesii

Date..................................

Location............................

Notes................................

....

....

....

❒ Rocky Mountain juniper

Sabina (=Juniperus) scopulorum

Date..................................

Location............................

Notes................................

....

....

....

❒ mountain muhly

Muhlenbergia montana

Date..................................

Location............................

Notes................................

....

....

....

❒ eastern fence lizard

Sceloporus undulatus

Date..................................

Location............................

Notes................................

....

....

....

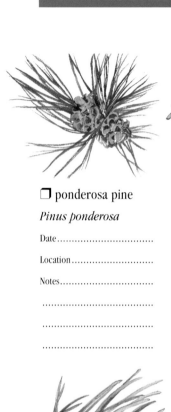

❒ lodgepole pine

Pinus contorta

Date..................................

Location............................

Notes................................

....

....

....

❒ quaking aspen

Populus tremuloides

Date..................................

Location............................

Notes................................

....

....

....

❒ wax currant

Ribes cereum

Date..................................

Location............................

Notes................................

....

....

....

❒ golden banner

Thermopsis divaricarpa

Date..................................

Location............................

Notes................................

....

....

❒ Steller's jay

Cyanocitta stelleri

Date..................................

Location............................

Notes................................

....

....

....

❏ **Williamson's sapsucker**
Sphyrapicus thyroideus
Date................................
Location............................
Notes................................
....
....

❏ **western bluebird**
Sialia mexicana
Date................................
Location............................
Notes................................
....
....
....

❏ **chipping sparrow**
Spizella passerina
Date................................
Location............................
Notes................................
....
....
....

❏ **red crossbill**
Loxia curvirostra
Date................................
Location............................
Notes................................
....
....
....

❏ **pygmy nuthatch**
Sitta pygmaea
Date................................
Location............................
Notes................................
....
....
....

❏ **western tanager**
Piranga ludoviciana
Date................................
Location............................
Notes................................
....
....
....

❏ **deer mouse**
Peromyscus maniculatus
Date................................
Location............................
Notes................................
....
....

❏ **porcupine**
Erethizon dorsatum
Date................................
Location............................
Notes................................
....
....

❏ **long-tailed weasel**
Mustela frenata
Date................................
Location ....
Notes................................
....
....
....

❏ **bushy-tailed woodrat**
Neotoma cinerea
Date................................
Location............................
Notes................................
....

❏ **golden-mantled ground squirrel**
Spermophilus lateralis
Date................................
Location............................
Notes................................
....
....

❏ **long-legged myotis**
Myotis volans
Date................................
Location............................
Notes................................
....

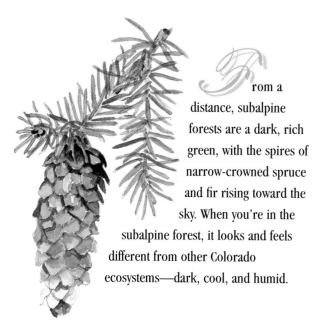

Engelmann spruce

From a distance, subalpine forests are a dark, rich green, with the spires of narrow-crowned spruce and fir rising toward the sky. When you're in the subalpine forest, it looks and feels different from other Colorado ecosystems—dark, cool, and humid.

Interrupted by highways, ski areas, and the occasional cabin, subalpine forests are nonetheless one of the most pristine ecosystems left in Colorado. The Silver Thread Scenic Byway is a 75-mile scenic drive through spectacular subalpine forest. It runs from South Fork, through Creede, and on to Lake City in southcentral Colorado's San Juan Mountains, crossing the Continental Divide.

Subalpine forests are cool even in the summer. For Colorado, they're very wet—with 30 or more inches of moisture each year. These forests get a lot of snowfall—76 inches of snow once fell in a 24-hour period at Silver Lake west of Boulder!—and even more snow blows down into the forest from the tundra above.

Dense forests of Engelmann spruce, subalpine fir, corkbark fir, quaking aspen, and limber and bristlecone pines grow at the highest elevations that will support trees in Colorado. Subalpine forests are found in mountain ranges throughout Colorado, from about 9,000 feet up to treeline. They occur above montane forests and just below the high, treeless alpine tundra.

Subalpine forest

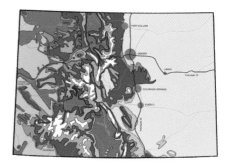

Subalpine forests aren't as diverse as many other ecosystems. Deep snow, long-lasting cold, and a short growing season mean that few animals live year-round in the subalpine. Elk come to graze in the open meadows on summer evenings, but in winter they move lower, where the snow isn't as deep.

The subalpine is too cold for most reptiles. Small mammals such as pine squirrels, red-backed voles, snowshoe hares, and deer mice are preyed on by red foxes and coyotes. Pine martens, found only in these high forests, climb trees and hunt small mammals, too. Wolverines and Canada lynxes, typical subalpine predators farther north, are extremely rare now—or extinct—in Colorado. Most subalpine birds eat bark insects and seeds. Pine grosbeaks, red crossbills, pine siskins, ruby-crowned kinglets, and hermit thrushes provide the subalpine forest's orchestra, punctuated by the woodpeckers' percussion. A few raptors—northern goshawks and the rare boreal owl—navigate in tight forest spaces to search out small mammals.

The tall spires of Engelmann spruce trees and subalpine firs and the big, flat feet of snowshoe hares are both adaptations to heavy snow. Snowshoe hares and long-tailed weasels change from summer brown to winter white in the fall, a great way to hide from predators in the snowy world of the subalpine forest. Other high forest animals, such as black bears, hibernate—sleeping away the long, cold winter.

Seldom-seen animals of the subalpine forest: (above) Canada lynx kitten, (right) wolverine, and (far right) pine marten

Forest, Dark and Deep

The red of Indian paintbrush mingles with the yellows of heart-leaved arnica, golden banner, and avalanche lilies—punctuated by the blue, white, and gold of columbines. The snows of winter have given rise to this summer show of wildflowers in a high mountain clearing. Surrounded by spruce, subalpine fir, and aspen, the clearing is a classic illustration of the brief bounty of summer in the subalpine forest. Mount Sneffels in the San Juan Mountains rises, majestic, in the background of this diorama scene. A male blue grouse, with his tail spread wide, tries to impress a well-camouflaged female perched on a log to the left.

San Juan Mountains

Notes & Observations in the subalpine forest, spring

Aspen Roles

This young female elk is chewing on aspen bark. Twigs and bark are part of the elks' winter diet—but they sometimes nibble in other seasons, too!

Aspen bark is high in vitamin K—which is essential for blood-clotting—and astringent salicin or salicylic acid—which is an ingredient in aspirin.

Indians used aspen bark to bandage cuts and broken limbs and to treat rheumatism, fevers, and pain.

Aspen Facts

❶. *An entire grove of aspen trees is just one individual! Usually an aspen grove grows from one network of roots, and all the trees in the grove are genetically identical—clones!*

❷ *Aspen root systems can exist for thousands of years (whether or not they produce trees). They lie dormant in the ground, waiting for fire, flood, or avalanche to clear a sunny space for them in the shady forest.*

❸ *When aspen roots sense that they can reach the sun at last, they send up "suckers" that become aspen trees.*

These chew marks were made over many years.

NOTE—Beavers also feed on aspen, and so do moose.

MAY—What creates the wonderful pattern of greens? Aspen groves among the conifers!

These aspens have filled in an old avalanche chute.

Succession Story

Avalanche! *A snowslide roars through an old-growth conifer forest, clearing a chute.*

5 years later, *aspen trees in the chute stand 6 feet high.*

80 years later, *the aspens are 60 feet tall. Spruce and fir trees are growing beneath them.*

200 years later, *the spruce and fir trees— now taller than the aspens—begin to shade the aspens out.*

300 years later, *the aspen trees are gone (the spruce and fir have succeeded them), but their roots remain—waiting beneath the surface for another day in the sun.*

Aspens are DECIDUOUS—they lose their leaves in the fall as a way to conserve moisture through the winter, when roots can't get water from the frozen ground.

(Aspens and cottonwoods are closely related.)

Which Tree Is Which?

Spruce, fir, and pine are EVERGREEN— they stay green year-round. These trees are conifers—they have cones and waxy needles and are especially well adapted to conserving moisture.

"Flat, friendly fir"

"Sharp, square spruce"

Spires of subalpine fir in the White River National Forest near Vail are covered with a thick blanket of snow, which will soon slide off in the sun's warmth.

Heart-leaved arnica and blueberry surround the trees, both upright and fallen, of this classic subalpine scene in central Colorado's Sawatch Range.

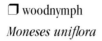

❑ woodnymph

Moneses uniflora

Date.................................

Location............................

Notes...............................

....

....

....

❑ blueberry

Vaccinium myrtillus

Date.................................

Location............................

Notes...............................

....

....

....

❑ Colorado columbine

Colorado's state flower

Aquilegia coerulea

Date.................................

Location............................

Notes...............................

....

....

....

❑ pine grosbeak

Pinicola enucleator

Date.................................

Location............................

Notes...............................

....

....

....

❑ Engelmann spruce

Picea engelmannii

Date.................................

Location............................

Notes...............................

....

....

....

❑ fairy slipper

Calypso bulbosa

Date.................................

Location............................

Notes...............................

....

....

....

❑ blue grouse

Dendragapus obscurus

Date.................................

Location............................

Notes...............................

....

....

....

❑ wild (Woods') rose

Rosa woodsii

Date.................................

Location............................

Notes...............................

....

....

....

❑ heart-leaved arnica

Arnica cordifolia

Date.................................

Location............................

Notes...............................

....

....

....

❑ subalpine fir

Abies lasiocarpa

Date.................................

Location............................

Notes...............................

....

....

....

❏ gray jay
Perisoreus canadensis

Date.................................

Location............................

Notes................................

....

....

....

❏ dark-eyed junco
Junco hyemalis

Date.................................

Location............................

Notes................................

....

....

....

❏ yellow-rumped
(Audubon's) warbler
Dendroica coronata

Date.................................

Location............................

Notes................................

....

....

....

❏ ruby-crowned
kinglet
Regulus calendula

Date.................................

Location............................

Notes................................

....

....

....

❏ red squirrel/pine
squirrel/chickaree
*Tamiasciurus
hudsonicus*

Date.................................

Location............................

Notes................................

....

....

....

❏ snowshoe hare
Lepus americanus

Date.................................

Location............................

Notes................................

....

....

....

❏ pine marten
Martes americanus

Date.................................

Location............................

Notes................................

....

....

....

❏ red-backed vole
*Clethrionomys
gapperi*

Date.................................

Location............................

Notes................................

....

....

❏ elk
Cervus elaphus

Date.................................

Location............................

Notes................................

....

....

....

❏ boreal toad
Bufo boreas

Date.................................

Location............................

Notes................................

....

....

....

Treeline is obvious from a distance—it's the ragged line where the trees stop and the tundra begins. Treeline occurs wherever high forests give way to tundra in Colorado's mountain ranges.

Up close, it's also obvious when you're at treeline—from the stunted, twisted shapes of the trees. These oddly shaped trees are called **krummholz,** from the German word for "crooked wood." Krummholz trees aren't any particular species; they can be subalpine fir, Engelmann spruce, bristlecone pine, or other trees. They just can't grow normally because of harsh winds and cold temperatures.

A view of treeline across Forest Canyon, Rocky Mountain National Park

Treeline lies at the highest edges of the subalpine forest, an elevation above which no trees can grow. It is colder, windier, and drier than the rest of the subalpine forest. Treeline is not actually an ecosystem in its own right. Instead it is a shared boundary—called an ecotone—between Colorado's two highest ecosystems. Treeline is, literally, a transition.

No species—plant or animal—is unique to treeline. It is inhabited by alpine species from above and forest species from below.

Treeline

The Mount Evans Highway, just off State Highway 103 south of Idaho Springs, is a wonderful place to cross treeline within an easy drive of Denver. A one-mile hiking trail off the road at Mount Goliath passes through a stand of gnarled bristlecone pines, some of Colorado's oldest trees.

Mount Goliath bristlecone pines

Life on the Edge

Temporarily lush, wildflowers in a rainbow of colors surround a twisted trunk where forest meets tundra, just below Loveland Pass west of Denver. The sculpted form of the bare, ancient subalpine fir—and the stunted younger sprouts at its base—are midsummer reminders of winter's relentless wind and lack of moisture. Remnant snowbanks still cover much of the tundra on adjacent peaks. A Clark's nutcracker keeps watch in this treeline diorama scene. A pine marten—shadowy predator of high mountain forests— peers from the evergreen needles, searching for lunch along the upper limits of tree cover.

Loveland Pass

Notes & Observations at treeline, summer

Life on the Edge

JULY — The vast sweep of the mountains and the jagged line where the trees finally peter out are awe-inspiring. And the weather shifts at the drop of a hat!

"Tree islands" appear far above the rest of the trees—testing the limits of tolerance. (If a tree gets a roothold in a natural windbreak or a sunny exposure, it, in turn, can shelter a few more trees . . .)

Wind Sculpts the Trees

N O T E — Snow, ice, and sand—hurled by howling winds—stunt and "flag" the Engelmann spruce, subalpine fir, bristlecone, and limber pine that struggle to grow here. The result is krummholz trees—German for "crooked wood."

Bristlecone pines in Colorado can live to be 2,000 years old, or more!

Such elegant, tortured shapes . . .

MATTED—Clumps of trees often grow together along the ground, huddled and woven together so tightly that you could walk on them!

FLAGGED—Strong wind and blowing ice crystals kill the growing buds on the windward side. (It's incredibly dry, cold, and windy above the snow—but underneath, it can be 50 degrees warmer.)

Ice Shaped the Land

AUGUST—Even in summer, it gets downright cold when a cloud crosses the sun. What was it like when glaciers filled these valleys?

Where the rivers of ice began, they scooped cirques from the mountains themselves. Ice carved broad, U-shaped valleys as it moved. Waterfalls, glacial lakes (or tarns), and moraines all indicate past glacial action.

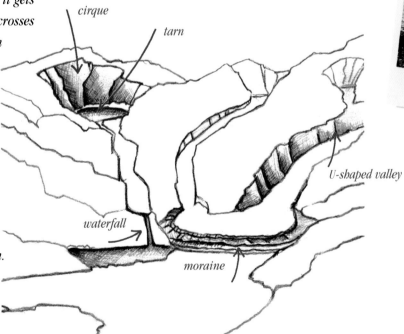

cirque

tarn

waterfall

U-shaped valley

moraine

August 3

Sunlight never warms this snowfield in the shadow of a hill, but wildflowers grow nearby.

The wind takes its toll, in bare trunks and brown needles, on subalpine firs at their limit of tolerance, growing near Cumberland Pass between Gunnison and Tincup.

Cast orange in the glow of sunset, trees and tundra
meet to form a sinuous line along Antora Peak in the
Sawatch Range south of Salida.

❏ bristlecone pine

Pinus aristata

Date.................................

Location...........................

Notes...............................

....

....

....

❏ Engelmann spruce

Picea engelmannii

Date.................................

Location...........................

Notes...............................

....

....

....

❏ flagged trees

Date.................................

Location...........................

Notes...............................

....

....

❏ matted tree "islands"

Date.................................

Location...........................

Notes...............................

....

❏ sedges

Carex spp.

Date.................................

Location...........................

Notes...............................

....

....

....

❏ limber pine

Pinus flexilus

Date.................................

Location...........................

Notes...............................

....

....

....

❏ subalpine fir

Abies lasiocarpa

Date.................................

Location...........................

Notes...............................

....

....

....

❏ twisted limbs

Date.................................

Location...........................

Notes...............................

....

....

....

❏ elephantella

Pedicularis groenlandica

Date.................................

Location...........................

Notes...............................

....

❏ rose crown

Clementsia rhodantha

Date.................................

Location...........................

Notes...............................

....

....

❏ marsh-marigold

Psychrophila (=Caltha)
leptosepala

Date.................................

Location...........................

Notes...............................

....

....

....

❏ white-crowned
sparrow

Zonotrichia leucophrys

Date.................................

Location...........................

Notes...............................

....

....

....

❏ elk

Cervus elaphus

Date.................................

Location...........................

Notes...............................

....

....

....

....

....

....

....

❏ pika

Ochotona princeps

Date.................................

Location...........................

Notes...............................

....

....

....

....

....

❏ yellow-bellied
marmot

Marmota flaviventris

Date.................................

Location...........................

Notes...............................

....

....

❏ bistort

Bistort bistortoides

Date.................................

Location...........................

Notes...............................

....

....

....

❏ white-tailed
ptarmigan

Lagopus leucurus

Date.................................

Location...........................

Notes...............................

....

....

....

❏ least chipmunk

Tamias minimus

Date.................................

Location...........................

Notes...............................

....

....

....

There's no mistaking an alpine tundra ecosystem. You're high above the trees, surrounded by open, windswept landscape. Rocks and ground may be patterned into polygon shapes from freeze-thaw frost action. In May or June, you might see "watermelon snow." These glistening snowbanks, painted pink, orange, or green by microscopic communities of algae, smell faintly like watermelon!

Sedges, grasses, low-growing willows, herbs, and mounded cushion plants are the only vegetation adapted to the conditions on the alpine tundra: extreme cold, intense solar radiation, slow soil formation, and a very short growing season. Winter temperatures in the tundra can reach 40 or 50 degrees below zero—without windchill! Although a lot of snow falls, much of it is driven by high winds into the subalpine forest below. It can—and does—snow any day of the year.

Alpine tundra is Colorado's highest ecosystem. There isn't a lot of tundra in Colorado in terms of square miles, but it is found throughout the state in all the high mountain ranges.

Alpine tundra

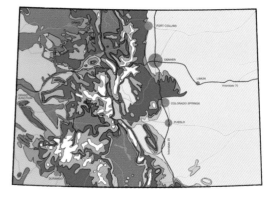

Even in summer, it's cold and windy on the alpine tundra—rarely above 60 degrees Fahrenheit—but on sunny, calm days you can feel your skin burning. Sunshine is especially intense in the alpine tundra, which is so high that the air up here is much thinner.

"Watermelon snow"

Alpine plant communities include meadows, snowbeds, talus fields, and fellfields. Fellfields, from the Gaelic word **fell,** meaning "rock," are groups of tundra plants that grow on windswept, rocky sites. Conditions there are as severe as in the desert. Fellfield plants are survivors—naturally tough and durable but easily disturbed by human intervention.

All the tundra's residents must cope with harsh conditions. Only a few animals live here all year. Like snowshoe hares, hardy white-tailed ptarmigans change color with the seasons to blend in with their surroundings. Yellow-bellied marmots hibernate for eight months of the year! Pikas don't hibernate but instead hide from the weather under the rocks in their boulderfield habitat. If the spring thaw is slow in coming, pikas just keep munching on the haypiles they collected and stored the summer before.

Moss campion

Elk in Rocky Mountain National Park

Like people, some animals are seasonal visitors. One of the tundra's most memorable sights is a herd of migrating elk or mountain sheep silhouetted against the sky, crossing high, open territory at the height of summer. The tundra in summer is a magical place, high above the world and wonderfully—if briefly—teeming with life, seemingly against all odds.

A summertime drive on Trail Ridge Road through Rocky Mountain National Park is one of the easiest and most spectacular ways to go from treeline into the tundra above. It's a treat to get out of your car at viewing areas along the way and to visit the alpine museum high in the mountains. Or, if you have a four-wheel-drive vehicle and a taste for adventure, try the 45-mile Alpine Loop Back Country Byway over Engineer and Cinnamon passes in the San Juan Mountains. You can reach the Alpine Loop from Lake City, Silverton, or Ouray.

Land of Extremes

Splashes of glorious color grace the hardy alpine plants that carpet the upper reaches of Longs Peak in Rocky Mountain National Park. The headwaters of a stream cut a channel through the tundra, beginning their long journey downstream. Glacier-formed boulders, hewn from the granite of the mountain, dominate this diorama scene. Even in July, patches of snow keep their hold in the shadows of the boulderfield and the peak beyond. A yellow-bellied marmot stands sentinel on his rock. Pikas and white-tailed ptarmigans—full-time residents of the alpine tundra—keep a sharp eye out for predators while foraging for their own food.

Longs Peak

Notes & Observations on the alpine tundra, spring & summer

Adaptations (like slow growth) help tundra plants survive but make them very vulnerable to human impact. A piece of litter can cover and kill plants in just 3 or 4 weeks! Recovery from disturbances—even footprints—takes many, many years.

(Not many animals actually live on the tundra all year.) May 20—At this time in spring, the ptarmigan are starting to change to their summer brown.

Earlier in May, still in their winter white, they blended right in.

Still winter on May 1

The tundra is as cold as the desert is hot, and almost as dry. The growing season is so short that alpine plants have to be really good at conserving energy and water.

❶ Almost all tundra plants are long-lived perennials, so they don't have to grow stems, leaves, flowers, and fruit all in one short season.

❷ Many hug the earth and are tightly matted—for protection against the wind and to take advantage of warmth near the ground. Some have hairy stems to trap heat and diffuse harmful solar radiation.

❸ Cushion plants are slow-growing, putting out only a few tiny leaves in a season.

❹ Like desert plants, some tundra plants are succulents. They can store water in their leaves. Waxy surfaces prevent evaporation.

*JULY—Pikas are great fun to watch—
they scamper, squeak, and chase each other like
kids playing. (Really, they're working—watching
for predators and harvesting, eating, and storing
sedges, grasses, and wildflowers.)*

*Pikas are closely related to rabbits and hares.
They're extremely well camouflaged to match their
boulderfield backdrop. Amazingly, they don't
hibernate.*

"Sedges have edges"

Coping with Conditions

*JULY—WOW! What colors!
Lots of alpine plants are brightly colored. Deeper
colors absorb more heat, which tundra plants
obviously need . . .*

*Anthocyanins—pigments that create red or
blue—actually convert light into heat.*

Moss campion

Alpine forget-me-not

Blossoms of bluebells and king's crown are almost lost among lichen-patterned rocks in a seemingly endless talus field at Mosquito Pass above South Park.

Snow lingers in every shadow and depression in this sweeping summer vista in the San Juan Mountains near Engineer Pass, between Lake City and Ouray.

Alone and craggy against the sky, Pilot Knob in the San Juan Mountains near Silverton overlooks a colorful profusion of summer wildflowers.

☐ **alpine avens**

Acomastylis rossii

Date.............................

Location ....

Notes............................

....

....

....

☐ **willow**

Salix spp.

Date.............................

Location ....

Notes............................

....

....

☐ **kobresia**

Kobresia myosuroides

Date.............................

Location ....

Notes............................

....

....

....

☐ **old-man-of-the-mountain**

Rydbergia grandiflora

Date.............................

Location ....

Notes............................

....

....

☐ **alpine spring beauty**

Claytonia megarhiza

Date.............................

Location ....

Notes............................

....

....

....

☐ **alpine sandwort**

Lidia (=Minuartia) obtusiloba

Date.............................

Location ....

Notes............................

....

....

....

☐ **king's crown**

Rhodiola integrifolia

Date.............................

Location ....

Notes............................

....

....

....

☐ **mountain dryad**

Dryas octopetala

Date.............................

Location ....

Notes............................

....

....

....

☐ **snowball saxifrage**

Micranthes rhomboidea

Date.............................

Location ....

Notes............................

....

....

....

☐ **alpine forget-me-not**

Eritrichum aretioides

Date.............................

Location ....

Notes............................

....

....

....

....

❒ moss campion

Silene acaulis

Date............................

Location ....

Notes...........................

....

....

....

....

....

❒ rosy finch

Leucosticte arctoa

Date............................

Location ....

Notes...........................

....

....

❒ pika

Ochotona princeps

Date............................

Location ....

Notes...........................

....

....

....

....

....

....

❒ northern pocket gopher

Thomomys talpoides

Date............................

Location ....

Notes...........................

....

....

....

....

....

❒ yellow-bellied marmot

Marmota flaviventris

Date............................

Location ....

Notes...........................

....

....

....

❒ American pipit

Anthus spinoletta

Date............................

Location ....

Notes...........................

....

....

....

❒ white-tailed ptarmigan

Lagopus leucurus

Date............................

Location ....

Notes...........................

....

....

....

....

❒ long-tailed weasel

Mustela frenata

Date............................

Location ....

Notes...........................

....

....

....

....

❒ bighorn sheep

Ovis canadensis

Date............................

Location ....

Notes...........................

....

....

....

....

....

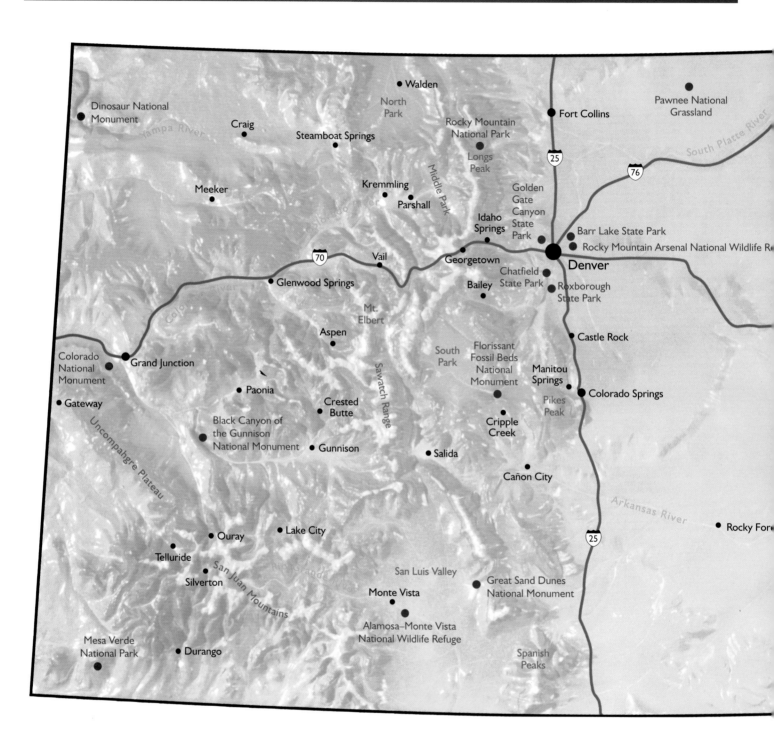

Walden
North Park
Dinosaur National Monument
Craig
Steamboat Springs
Rocky Mountain National Park
Pawnee National Grassland
Fort Collins
South Platte River
Tampa River
Longs Peak
Meeker
Kremmling
Parshall
Middle Park
Golden Gate Canyon State Park
Idaho Springs
Barr Lake State Park
Rocky Mountain Arsenal National Wildlife R
70
Vail
Georgetown
Denver
Glenwood Springs
Chatfield State Park
Bailey
Roxborough State Park
Mt. Elbert
Aspen
Castle Rock
Colorado National Monument
Grand Junction
South Park
Florissant Fossil Beds National Monument
Manitou Springs
Gateway
Paonia
Sawatch Range
Colorado Springs
Pikes Peak
Black Canyon of the Gunnison National Monument
Crested Butte
Cripple Creek
Gunnison
Salida
Cañon City
Arkansas River
Rocky For
Lake City
Ouray
Telluride
San Juan Mountains
San Luis Valley
Great Sand Dunes National Monument
Silverton
Monte Vista
Mesa Verde National Park
Durango
Alamosa–Monte Vista National Wildlife Refuge
Spanish Peaks
Uncompahgre Plateau
25
76

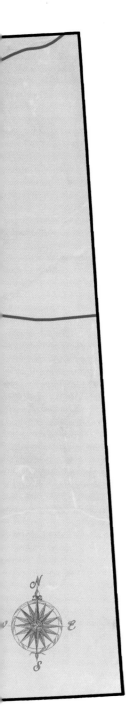

Activities for All Seasons

*C*olorado has beautiful places to explore any time of the year. This is by no means a complete list of sights to see and things to do, but it should help get you started.

Year-round

Come see for yourself the spectacular dioramas featured in this book. (They're even better in person!) In addition to the *Explore Colorado* exhibition on the third floor, the **Denver Museum of Natural History** features exhibits about animals, dinosaurs, the human body, and much more. For information, call (303) 322-7009.

Haven't had much luck viewing wildlife in the wild? Then visit the **Denver Zoo** to see animals from Colorado and the rest of the world. The zoo is open every day of the year. For recorded information, call (303) 331-4100.

For some practice identifying plants, spend a few hours at the **Denver Botanic Gardens.** Plants in the wild don't have name tags next to them like the ones here do! The Plains Garden, the Gates Garden, and the Rock Alpine Garden all include plants you'll see in your travels. For recorded information, call (303) 331-4000.

Spring

Thousands of sandhill cranes and a few endangered whooping cranes (and many other feathered friends) migrate through the San Luis Valley each spring. A fabulous place to see them is at the **Monte Vista National Wildlife Refuge.** The cranes arrive here about the end of February and head north by April 1. The number of visiting cranes peaks about March 10. For information, call the refuge's administrative offices at (719) 589-4021 or write to Alamosa/Monte Vista National Wildlife Refuge Complex, 9383 El Rancho Lane, Alamosa, CO 81101.

The **Monte Vista Crane Festival** honors these temporary guests in mid-March and includes educational seminars about wildlife, bus tours of the nearby refuge, and wildlife art shows. For information, call the Monte Vista Chamber of Commerce at (719) 852-2731 or write to them at 1035 Park Ave., Monte Vista, CO 81144.

Sandhill cranes at Monte Vista National Wildlife Refuge

Wildflowers in the San Juan Mountains

To find out where wildflowers are blooming any week during April through July, call the **Wild Hot Line** at 1-800-354-4595 sponsored by the Bureau of Land Management.

See both grassland and riparian areas at the **Pawnee National Grassland.** The wildlife viewing here includes pronghorn herds, raptors, and a self-guided birding tour complete with a species checklist. For information, call the U.S. Forest Service at (970) 353-5004 or write to Pawnee National Grassland, 660 O St., Greeley, CO 80631.

One of Colorado's best bird-watching spots is located just south of Denver at **Chatfield State Park.** More than 300 species have been seen here, and viewing blinds and scopes at the heron rookery offer a great chance to view these water birds (and others) up close. For information, call the park at (303) 791-7275.

Young bald eagles

Barr Lake State Park is yet another bird-watcher's paradise near Denver, nesting bald eagles being the big draw here. The riparian and grassland areas attract small mammals, reptiles, and some 350 bird species. The park is located just off Interstate 76 at Exit 23. For information, call the park's Wildlife Center at (303) 659-6005.

Summer

Wondering what Colorado's ecosystems were like 35 million years ago? Plan a trip to **Florissant Fossil Beds National Monument.** Rock formations preserve the fossilized remains of palm trees, redwoods, insects, fish, and other organisms that lived here. For information, call the park's Visitor Center at (719) 748-3253 or write to them at P.O. Box 185, Florissant, CO 80816.

Fossilized crane fly

Check out the summer blossoms in the official wildflower capital of Colorado. The **Crested Butte Wildflower Festival** in early July offers daily guided hikes to view the local flora. Drawing, photography, and cooking classes are just some of the other events you can attend. For information, call the Crested Butte Chamber of Commerce at 1-800-545-4505 or write to Crested Butte Wildflower Festival, P.O. Box 216, Crested Butte, CO 81224.

Rocky Mountain National Park is worth a visit every season of the year. In summer, you can take **Trail Ridge Road** (or the one-way, dirt **Old Fall River Road** if you and your car are feeling more adventurous) to the **Alpine Visitor Center** (elevation 11,796 feet). You may need a jacket up here even in August. If high altitudes don't agree with you, stay down at the **Moraine Park Museum** and learn how this area was formed by glaciers. For information, call the park at (970) 586-1206 or write to Superintendent, Rocky Mountain National Park, Estes Park, CO 80517. Recorded information, including weather and road conditions, is available by calling (970) 586-1333.

Trail Ridge Road in Rocky Mountain National Park

Located on Highway 285 fifteen miles west of Bailey, **Wilderness On Wheels** makes nature totally accessible to people in wheelchairs. Campsites, rest rooms, a creek-side nature trail, and (eventually) a trail to the top of Twin Peaks are available free of charge from mid-April through mid-October. Reservations are required. For information, call Wilderness On Wheels at (303) 988-2212 or write to them at 7125 W. Jefferson Ave., Suite 155, Lakewood, CO 80235.

The **Vail Nature Center** presents exhibits and guided nature walks to help you discover the plants and wildlife found in this part of Colorado. The center is located at the east end of town and is open daily from May to September. For information, call them at (970) 479-2291.

These may not all be native plants, but they do grow here. Honor your favorite at one of these festivals:

• **Strawberry Days in Glenwood Springs**—Colorado's oldest civic festival—is held the third weekend in June and offers free strawberries and ice cream for all! For information, call the Glenwood Springs Chamber Resort Association at (970) 945-6589 or write to them at 1102 Grand Ave., Glenwood Springs, CO 81601.

• **Paonia Cherry Days** in early July celebrates the area's cherry harvest. For information, call the Paonia Chamber of Commerce at (970) 527-3886 or write to them at P.O. Box 366, Paonia, CO 81428.

• **Watermelon Day** at the Arkansas Valley Fair in mid-August celebrates the valley's melon harvest. For information, call the Rocky Ford Chamber of Commerce at (719) 254-7483 or write to them at 105 N. Main St., Rocky Ford, CO 81067.

• **Telluride Mushroom Conference** in late August is for folks with more than a passing interest in these fungi. For information, call Telluride Visitor Services at (970) 728-4431 inside Colorado or 1-800-525-3455 out of state, or write to Fungophile, Inc., P.O. Box 480503, Denver, CO 80248.

Colorado mushrooms

Autumn

Aspen trees are the stars of Colorado's fall foliage. In September and October, **Colorfest** in the Four Corners area provides various activities (such as art shows, an antique car show, and raft races) to supplement your tree-watching. For information, call the Durango Area Chamber Resort Association at (970) 247-0312 or 1-800-GO-DURANGO, or write to them at P.O. Box 2587, Durango, CO 81302.

Fall colors usually reach their peak in **Rocky Mountain National Park** in September. A drive up **Trail Ridge Road** takes you through several ecosystems and lots of spectacular vistas. The road closes for the winter sometime in October, depending on snowfall. If you're in the park at dusk in mid-September through October, you might hear the wild symphony of **male elk bugling** as they try to attract a mate. For information, call the park at (970) 586-1206 or write to Superintendent, Rocky Mountain National Park, Estes Park, CO 80517. Recorded information, including weather and road conditions, is available by calling (970) 586-1333.

Male elk

To see the fall foliage in the central part of the state, head to Cripple Creek for **Aspen Jeep Tours.** During the last two weekends in September and the first weekend in October, volunteers take you from the sign-up point in City Park for a free ride through the nearby mountains. For information, call the Cripple Creek Chamber of Commerce at (719) 689-2169 or 1-800-526-8777, or write to them at P.O. Box 650, Cripple Creek, CO 80813.

Fall colors near
Cripple Creek

The grasses of northwest Colorado lured sheep ranchers here long ago. During the second weekend in September, the town of Meeker celebrates this part of its heritage with the **Meeker Classic Sheep Dog Championship Trials.** Amazing herding dogs and their owners take on the local sheep. For information, call the Meeker Chamber of Commerce at (970) 878-5510 or write to them at P.O. Box 869, Meeker, CO 81641.

Roxborough State Park south of Denver is a good bird-watching site year-round and offers the chance to visit a transitional environment between the plains and the foothills. For information, call the park's Visitor Center at (303) 973-3959.

Ferruginous hawk

Winter

Not all birds fly south to the tropics this time of year. Various raptors, including bald eagles, spend the winter at the **Rocky Mountain Arsenal National Wildlife Refuge,** feeding on the local prairie dog and cottontail rabbit populations. The Eagle Watch viewing blind is open from December through March, or you can call ahead to inquire about tours. The refuge is located northeast of Denver. For information, call (303) 289-0232.

On your way to the slopes, stop at the **Georgetown Bighorn Viewing Site.** Bighorn sheep often forage on the hillside across the highway. Even if you don't catch a glimpse of the animals, you'll get a great view of prime bighorn sheep habitat through the coin-operated viewing scopes. Take Exit 228 off Interstate 70. For information, call the town of Georgetown at (303) 569-2555 or at 623-6882 in the Denver metro area.

Bighorn sheep

Didn't make it to **Rocky Mountain National Park** for the aspens and the elk? Go anyway. Rangers lead ski tours, snowshoe excursions, bird walks, and other programs throughout the winter, and the Headquarters and Kawuneeche Visitor Centers remain open year-round. Call the park at (970) 586-1206 to find out what events are scheduled or write to Superintendent, Rocky Mountain National Park, Estes Park, CO 80517. Recorded information, including weather and road conditions, is available by calling (970) 586-1333.

If you're out cross-country skiing or snowshoeing, watch for animal tracks in the snow. Lots of birds and mammals stay active during the winter.

Andrews, Robert, and Robert Righter. *Colorado Birds*. Denver: Denver Museum of Natural History, 1992.

Armstrong, David M. *Rocky Mountain Mammals: A Handbook of Mammals of Rocky Mountain National Park and Vicinity.* Boulder, Colo.: Colorado Associated University Press and Rocky Mountain Nature Association, 1987.

Benedict, Audrey D. *A Sierra Club Naturalist's Guide to the Southern Rockies.* San Francisco: Sierra Club Books, 1991.

Benyus, Janine M. *The Field Guide to Wildlife Habitats of the Western United States.* New York: Simon and Schuster, 1989.

Burt, William H., and Richard P. Grossenheider. *A Field Guide to the Mammals.* Boston: Houghton Mifflin Company, 1964.

Carter, Jack L. *Trees and Shrubs of Colorado.* Boulder, Colo.: Johnson Books, 1988.

Chronic, Halka. *Roadside Geology of Colorado.* Missoula, Mont.: Mountain Press Publishing Company, 1980.

Craighead, John J., Frank C. Craighead, and Ray J. Davis. *A Field Guide to Rocky Mountain Wildflowers.* The Peterson Field Guide Series. Boston: Houghton Mifflin Company, 1963.

Cooper, Ann C., Ann B. Armstrong, and Carol A. Kampert. *The WildWatch Book: Ideas, Activities, and Projects for Exploring Colorado's Front Range.* Denver: Denver Museum of Natural History and Roberts Rinehart Publishers, 1990.

Duft, Joseph F., and Robert K. Moseley. *Alpine Wildflowers of the Rocky Mountains.* Missoula, Mont.: Mountain Press Publishing Company, 1989.

Fitzgerald, James P., Carron A. Meaney, and David M. Armstrong. *Mammals of Colorado.* Niwot, Colo.: University Press of Colorado and Denver Museum of Natural History, 1994.

Gray, Mary Taylor. *Colorado Wildlife Viewing Guide.* Helena and Billings, Mont.: Falcon Press, 1990.

Halfpenny, James. *A Field Guide to Mammal Tracking in Western America.* Boulder, Colo.: Johnson Books, 1986.

Hammerson, Geoffrey A. *Amphibians and Reptiles in Colorado.* Denver: Colorado Division of Wildlife, 1982.

Keen, Richard A. *Skywatch: The Western Weather Guide.* Golden, Colo.: Fulcrum, Inc., 1987.

Leopold, Aldo. *A Sand County Almanac, and Sketches Here and There.* New York: Oxford University Press, 1949.

Mutel, Cornelia F., and John C. Emerick. *From Grassland to Glacier: The Natural History of Colorado and the Surrounding Region.* Boulder, Colo.: Johnson Books, 1992.

National Geographic Society. *Field Guide to the Birds of North America.* Washington, D.C.: National Geographic Society, 1987.

Nelson, Ruth A. *Handbook of Rocky Mountain Plants.* Fourth edition. Denver: Denver Museum of Natural History and Roberts Rinehart Publishers, 1992.

Pyle, Robert M. *The Audubon Society Field Guide to North American Butterflies.* New York: Alfred A. Knopf, 1981.

Rennicke, Jeff. *Colorado Wildlife.* Helena and Billings, Mont.: Falcon Press, 1990.

Weber, William A. *Colorado Flora: Eastern Slope.* Boulder, Colo.: Colorado Associated University Press, 1990.

Weber, William A. *Colorado Flora: Western Slope.* Boulder, Colo.: Colorado Associated University Press, 1987.

Zwinger, Ann H., and Beatrice E. Willard. *Land Above the Trees: A Guide to American Alpine Tundra.* New York: Harper and Row, 1972.

Pallid bat

Photography

John Fielder © 1995: front cover, pages 1, 3, 5, 6, 28 (top), 29, 38 (bottom), 39, 48, 49, 58, 59, 68, 69, 77 (below), 78, 88, 89, 98, 99, 108, 109

Wendy Shattil/Bob Rozinski © 1995: pages 7, 8, 22 (top), 23, 28 (bottom), 32 (left), 33, 38 (top), 43 (top left, bottom), 52 (right), 53, 56 (top right), 63 (right, bottom), 73 (top), 77 (above), 79, 83, 92 (bottom), 93 (right), 102 (left), 103, 114–121

Denver Museum of Natural History Photo Archives: pages 17 (top), 19 (top left), 37, 86, 97, 106 (center)

Denver Museum of Natural History photographers:
Gary Hall: 34–35, 44–45, 54–55, 64–65, 74–75, 84–85, 94–95, 104–105
David McGrath: 76 (center)
Richard Stum: 24–25
Rick Wicker: 7, 26, 27, 36, 46, 47, 56 (bottom left, center), 57, 66, 76 (bottom left, bottom right, right center), 87, 96, 106 (bottom right), 107

Illustrations

Elizabeth Biesiot: pages 11 (top), 12 (bottom), 13, 14, 15 (bottom), 19 (saguaro cactus), 31 (pronghorn, thirteen-lined ground squirrel), 40 (big sagebrush), 41 (desert cottontail, Ord's kangaroo rat), 50 (mountain-mahogany), 51 (mountain cottontail, pallid bat, mountain lion, ringtail), 61 (striped skunk, muskrat, meadow vole, white-tailed deer), 63, 70 (mountain-mahogany), 71 (deer mouse, rock squirrel), 76 (top right), 77, 81 (red crossbill, deer mouse, long-tailed weasel, bushy-tailed woodrat, golden-mantled ground squirrel, long-legged myotis), 82 (top left), 90 (Engelmann spruce, subalpine fir), 91 (red squirrel, pine marten, red-backed vole), 100 (Engelmann spruce, subalpine fir), 101 (least chipmunk), 111 (northern pocket gopher, long-tailed weasel), 123

Steve Elliott: pages 10, 11 (bottom), 12 (top), 15 (top), 18 (bottom), 26, 27, 31 (horned lark, western meadowlark, golden eagle, red-tailed hawk, black-tailed jackrabbit, black-tailed prairie dog), 36–37, 41 (sage grouse, coyote), 43, 46, 47, 50 (collared lizard, piñon jay), 51 (piñon mouse), 56 (right), 57, 61 (great blue heron, beaver), 71 (wild turkey, gray fox, western spotted skunk, mule deer, coyote), 73 (bottom), 76 (top left), 81 (porcupine), 86 (left), 87, 92, 96, 97, 100 (flagged trees, twisted limbs, matted tree), 101 (white-tailed ptarmigan, elk, pika, yellow-bellied marmot), 106, 107, 110 (alpine forget-me-not), 111 (moss campion, white-tailed ptarmigan, pika, yellow-bellied marmot, bighorn sheep), back cover

Dick Hanna: 112–113

Jackie McFarland: pages 4, 9, 18 (top), 22 (bottom), 30, 31 (bullsnake), 32 (bottom right), 40 (all except big sagebrush), 41 (western rattlesnake), 42 (top left), 50 (all plants except mountain-mahogany; side-blotched lizard), 52 (top left), 56 (left), 60, 61 (both snakes), 62 (top left), 70 (all plants except mountain-mahogany and needle-and-thread; bullsnake), 80 (all except Steller's jay), 90 (blueberry, wild rose, Colorado columbine, heart-leaved arnica, woodnymph, fairy slipper), 100 (limber pine, elephantella, rose crown), 101 (marsh-marigold, bistort), 110 (all except alpine forget-me-not), 125, back flap

Lupine

Denver Museum of Natural History Archives: page 11 (top left)

William C. Dilger: page 81 (western bluebird)

Donald R. Eckelberry: page 31 (lark bunting)

Owen J. Gromme: page 90 (blue grouse)

David M. Henry: page 71 (lazuli bunting)

Al Kreml: pages 61 (yellow warbler), 91 (yellow-rumped warbler)

Donald L. Malick: pages 41 (Brewer's sparrow, canyon towhee, sage thrasher), 51 (blue-gray gnatcatcher, bushtit, common poorwill, plain titmouse), 61 (American dipper), 71 (green-tailed towhee, rufous-sided towhee), 81 (chipping sparrow, western tanager, Williamson's sapsucker), 90 (pine grosbeak), 91 (dark-eyed junco, ruby-crowned kinglet), 101 (white-crowned sparrow), 111 (American pipit, rosy finch)

Richard A. Parks: page 71 (Virginia's warbler)

Earl L. Poole: pages 31 (red-tailed hawk), 51 (American kestrel)

Charles L. Ripper: pages 71 (scrub jay), 80 (Steller's jay), 91 (gray jay)

Agnus H. Shortt: page 81 (pygmy nuthatch)

Wayne Trimm: page 61 (belted kingfisher, great horned owl)

Index

Abert's squirrel, 19, 73, 77
acorn, 65, 67
Alamosa-Monte Vista
   National Wildlife Refuge,
   112, 114
alders, 53
algae, 102
alkali, 32
Alpine Loop Back Country
   Byway, 103
Alpine Visitor Center,
   Rocky Mountain National
   Park, 103, 116
alpine avens, 110
alpine forget-me-not, 107,
   110
alpine sandwort, 110
alpine spring beauty, 110
alpine tundra, 20–21, 82,
   92, 95, 102–111
American crow, 73
American dipper, 61
American kestrel, 51
American pipit, 111
amphibians, 53
anthocyanins, 107
Antora Peak, 99
arrowleaf balsam-root, 40
Aspen (town), 58, 112
aspen (tree), 18, 19, 58,
   72, 75, 85, 86, 87, 118,
   119
Aspen Jeep Tours, 119
aspen root systems, 86
avalanche, 87
avalanche lilies, 85

badger, 23
Bailey, 112, 117
bald eagle, 115, 120

balsam-root, 35, 40
bandtailed pigeon, 65, 67
barley, 26
Barr Lake, 53
Barr Lake State Park, 112,
   115
Bear Creek Canyon
   Regional Park, 62
beaver, 4, 5, 52, 53, 61, 86
beetles, 67
belted kingfisher, 61
big sagebrush, 40
bighorn sheep, 43, 103,
   111, 121
biodiversity, 9, 11,
bison, 26, 27
bistort, 101
bitterbrush, 50
bittercress, 60
black bear, 43, 63, 83
Black Canyon of the
   Gunnison National
   Monument, 112
Black Forest, 72
black-billed magpie, 73
black-crowned night
   heron, 55, 57
black-footed ferret, 27
black-tailed jackrabbit, 31,
   32, 41
black-tailed prairie dog, 31
blue grama, 22, 26, 30
blue grouse, 85, 90
blue spruce, 52
blue-gray gnatcatcher, 45,
   51
bluebells, 108
blueberry, 87, 90
bobcat, 63
boreal owl, 83
boreal toad, 53, 91
Boulder, 42

box-elder, 52, 60
Brewer's sparrow, 41
bristlecone pine, 19, 82,
   92, 93, 96, 100
broad-leaved cattail, 60
broom snakeweed, 30
brown towhee, 45
buffalograss, 22, 26, 30
bullsnake, 31, 70, 73
bulrushes, 52, 60
burrowing owl, 23
bushtit, 45, 51
bushy-tailed woodrat, 81

Canada lynx, 83
Cañon City, 112
canyon towhee, 41
Castle Rock, 69
cattails, 52, 53, 58, 60
cattle, 26, 27
Chatfield Reservoir, 53, 55
Chatfield State Park, 112,
   115
chickaree, 91
chiming bells, 35
chinook winds, 13
chipmunk, 47, 63, 73
chipping sparrow, 81
chlorophyll, 66
Cinnamon Pass, 103
cirque, 97
claret cup, 45
Clark's nutcracker, 95
climate, 12–13, 22, 32, 42,
   52, 62, 72, 82, 93, 102
collared lizard, 50
Colorado columbine, 90
Colorado National
   Monument, 43, 112
Colorado Plateau, 49
Colorado Springs, 42, 62,
   72, 73, 75, 112

Colorfest, 118
columbines, 85, 90
common poorwill, 51
corkbark fir, 82
corn, 26, 67
cottontail rabbit, 120
cottonwoods, 10, 39, 52,
   55, 56, 57, 58, 87
coyote, 18, 23, 41, 63, 71,
   83
Craig, 33, 112
Creede, 82
Crested Butte, 112, 116
Crested Butte Wildflower
   Festival, 116
crickets, 67
Cripple Creek, 112, 119
Cumberland Pass, 98
cushion plants, 102, 106

dark-eyed junco, 73, 91
deciduous, 87
deer mouse, 47, 63, 71,
   81, 83
Denver, 10, 11, 26, 53, 62,
   73, 93, 95
Denver Botanic Gardens,
   113
Denver Museum of Natural
   History, 8, 9, 16, 17, 18,
   21, 113
Denver Zoo, 113
desert cottontail, 41
Dinosaur National
   Monument, 112
dippers, 53, 61
Dominguez Canyon, 58
Douglas-fir, 18, 19, 72, 76,
   80
dragonflies, 53
ducks, 53
Durango, 112, 118

eastern fence lizard, 40, 80
ecosystem, 9, 15, 16, 17,
   21
ecotone, 93
elephantella, 100
elevation, 11, 13, 22, 32,
   52, 62, 72, 82
elk, 43, 83, 86, 91, 101,
   103, 118
Elkhead Mountains, 35, 36
Engineer Pass, 103, 108
Engelmann spruce, 82, 83,
   90, 92, 96, 100
evergreen, 42, 75, 87

fairy slipper, 77, 90
fellfields, 103
ferret, 23
ferruginous hawk, 120
fir, 82, 87
fish, 53, 57
flagged trees, 97, 100
flammulated owl, 73
Florissant Fossil Beds
   National Monument, 73,
   112, 116
Forest Canyon, 92
Fort Collins, 42, 112
Four Corners area, 49, 118
four-winged saltbush, 40
foxes, 23, 52, 63
fringed sage, 30
frogs, 53, 57, 60

galleta grass, 40
Gateway, 38, 112
generalists, 19
Georgetown, 112, 121
Georgetown Bighorn
   Viewing Site, 121
glacier, 97, 116

Glenwood Springs, 53, 112, 117

Golden, 73

golden banner, 80, 85

golden eagle, 31, 41

Golden Gate Canyon State Park, 112

golden-mantled ground squirrel, 63, 81

gopher, 23

Grand Junction, 43, 112

grasses, 22, 23, 25, 26, 36, 58, 72, 102, 119

grasshoppers, 67

grassland, 20–21, 22–31, 42, 115

gray fox, 71

gray jay, 91

greasewood, 32, 40

Great Sand Dunes National Monument, 39, 112

great blue heron, 53, 55, 57, 61

great horned owl, 61

great plains toad, 53

green-tailed towhee, 71

ground squirrels, 63

Gunnison, 98, 112

Gunnison Basin, 32

Gunnison National Forest, 6

Hanging Lake, 53

Headquarters Visitor Center, Rocky Mountain National Park, 121

heart-leaved arnica, 85, 89, 90

herbs, 102

hermit thrush, 83

herons, 53, 57, 115

hogback, 66

Holly, 11

horned lark, 22, 25, 27, 31

Idaho Springs, 93, 112

Indian paintbrush, 85

Indian ricegrass, 50

Indians, 26, 86

indigo bunting, 63

insects, 23, 45, 47, 57, 67, 83

jackrabbits, 23, 31, 47

Jarre Canyon, 65, 66

Jefferson County Open Space, 73

Junegrass, 50

juniper berries, 43, 46

juniper seeds, 47

juniper trees, 42, 45, 46, 49, 50

kangaroo rats, 23

Kawuneeche Visitor Center, Rocky Mountain National Park, 121

Keota, 23

king's crown, 108, 110

kobresia, 110

Kremmling, 33, 112

krummholz, 92, 96

La Garita-Penitente Canyon area, 43

Lake City, 82, 103, 108, 112

lark bunting, 25, 28, 31

lazuli bunting, 71

least chipmunk, 101

leaves, color change of, 66

lek, 37

lichens, 45, 108

lifezones, 8, 14

limber pine, 82, 96, 100

lizards, 45, 50

lodgepole pine, 18, 19, 72, 78, 80

long-legged myotis, 81

long-tailed weasel, 81, 83, 111

Longs Peak, 105, 106, 112

Lookout Mountain Nature Center, 73

Loveland Pass, 95, 96

lupine, 70, 78, 125

Manitou Springs, 62, 112

marsh-marigold, 101

matted tree islands, 97, 100

meadow vole, 61

Meeker, 58, 112, 119

Meeker Classic Sheep Dog Championship Trials, 119

Merriam, C. Hart, 8, 14

Mesa Verde National Park, 45, 46, 112

mice, 23, 63

Middle Park, 22, 32, 112

montane forest, 19, 20–21, 42, 82

montane shrubland, 20–21, 62–71

Monte Vista, 112, 114

Monte Vista Crane Festival, 114

moose, 86

moraine, 97

Moraine Park Museum, Rocky Mountain National Park, 116

Morrison, 62

Mosquito Pass, 108

moss campion, 103, 107, 111

Mount Elbert, 11, 112

Mount Evans, 55

Mount Evans Highway, 93

Mount Goliath, 93

Mount Sneffels, 85

Mount Zirkel Wilderness, 59

mountain cottontail, 51

mountain dryad, 110

mountain lion, 51, 63

mountain-mahogany, 50, 62, 63, 70

mountain muhly, 80

mountain plover, 25, 27

mule deer, 18, 32, 43, 46, 67, 71, 73, 74–75, 76, 79

musk thistle, 28

muskrat, 56, 61

needle-and-thread, 30, 70

North Park, 32, 112

northern flicker, 77

northern goshawk, 83

northern pocket gopher, 111

oats, 26

Old Fall River Road, Rocky Mountain National Park, 116

old man's beard, 77

old-man-of-the-mountain, 110

one-seed juniper, 50

orange lichen, 63

Ord's kangaroo rat, 33, 41

Ouray, 103, 108, 112

Owl's Canyon, 42

paintbrush, 40

pallid bat, 51, 123

Paonia, 112, 117

Paonia Cherry Days, 117

parks (high grasslands), 22

Parry's primrose, 59

Parshall, 53, 112

parsnip, 60

pasque flower, 7

Pawnee Buttes, 3, 4, 23, 25

Pawnee National Grassland, 3, 4, 23, 24–25, 26, 113, 115

perennials, 106

pika, 18, 101, 103, 105, 107, 111

Pikes Peak, 75, 112

Pilot Knob, 109

pine grosbeak, 83, 90

pine marten, 83, 91, 95

pine siskin, 73, 83

pine squirrel, 83, 91

piñon jay, 18, 43, 45, 47, 50

piñon mouse, 43, 47, 51

piñon nuts, 43, 46, 47

piñon pine, 42, 43, 45, 46, 47, 48, 49, 50

piñon-juniper woodland, 20–21, 42–51

plain titmouse, 51

plains garter snake, 61

plover, 23

ponderosa pine, 19, 69, 72, 73, 76, 77, 79, 80

porcupine, 73, 79, 81

prairie coneflower, 9, 22, 30

prairie dog, 22, 23, 26, 27, 31, 120

prairie sandreed, 28

prickly pear cactus, 22, 25, 30, 45

pronghorn, 23, 26, 27, 31, 32, 33, 38, 43, 115

ptarmigan, 19

pygmy forest, 42, 43

pygmy nuthatch, 73, 77, 81

quail, 45, 47, 63
quaking aspen, 80, 82

rabbitbrush, 32, 33, 36, 39, 40, 46
Rampart Range, 73, 76
rattlesnakes, 23, 30, 41
red crossbill, 77, 81, 83
red fox, 83
Red Rocks Park, 62
red squirrel, 91
red-backed vole, 83, 91
red-tailed hawk, 31
red-winged blackbird, 53
reptiles, 57, 73, 83, 115
rice, 26
ringtail, 47, 51
riparian land, 20–21, 52–61, 115
rock squirrel, 47, 67, 71
Rocky Ford, 113, 117
Rocky Mountain Arsenal National Wildlife Refuge, 112, 120
Rocky Mountain juniper, 80
Rocky Mountain National Park, 11, 92, 103, 105, 112, 116, 118, 121
rookery, 55, 57
rose crown, 100
rose hips, 67
rosy finch, 111
Roxborough State Park, 112, 119
ruby-crowned kinglet, 83, 91
rufous-sided towhee, 63, 71

rye, 26

sage grouse, 33, 34–35, 36–37, 41
sage sparrow, 33
sage thrasher, 33, 41
sagebrush, 18, 32, 36, 40
sagebrush lizard, 40
sagebrush vole, 32
saguaro cactus, 19
salamanders, 53, 57, 60
Salida, 99, 112
saltbush, 32, 40
San Isabel National Forest, 68
San Juan Mountains, 82, 85, 86, 103, 108, 109, 112, 115
San Luis Valley, 32, 33, 38, 43, 58, 112, 114
sand sagebrush, 28
sandhill crane, 114
Sawatch Range, 78, 89, 99, 112
Sawatch River, 4, 5
scaled quail, 45, 63
scarlet gilia, 70
scrub jay, 63, 64, 65, 67, 71
scrub oak, 62, 65, 67, 68, 69, 70
sedges, 52, 60, 100, 102, 107
semidesert shrubland, 20–21, 32–41, 42
serviceberry, 62, 70
sharp-tailed grouse, 65, 67
sheep, 26, 119
shrubs, 32, 33, 36, 38, 72

side-blotched lizard, 50
Silver Lake, 82
silver sage, 30
Silver Thread Scenic Byway, 82
Silverton, 103, 109, 112
skunkbrush, 65, 70
smooth sumac, 70
snowball saxifrage, 110
snowberry, 70
snowshoe hare, 83, 91
snowy egret, 55, 57
South Fork, 82
South Park, 22, 108, 112
South Platte River 28, 53, 55, 56
Spanish Peaks, 68, 112
specialists, 19
spiny, softshelled turtle, 56
spotted skunk, 63
spruce, 82, 85, 87
squirrel tail, 40
Steamboat Springs, 112
Steller's jay, 73, 74, 75, 77, 80
Strawberry Days, Glenwood Springs, 117
striped chorus frog, 60
striped skunk, 61
subalpine fir, 82, 83, 85, 88, 90, 92, 95, 96, 98, 100
subalpine forest, 19, 20–21, 72, 82–91, 93
succulents, 106
sugarcane, 26
Sugarloaf Campground Boardwalk, 53
sumac, 62, 65, 70
sunflowers, 33

swift fox, 23

talus field, 103, 108
tarantula, 45
tarn, 97
Telluride, 112, 117
Telluride Mushroom Conference, 117
thirteen-lined ground squirrel, 31
tiger salamander, 60
Tincup, 98
Trail Ridge Road, Rocky Mountain National Park, 11, 103, 116, 118
tree island, 96
treeline, 20–21, 92–101
trout, 53

U-shaped valley, 97
Unaweep Canyon, 38
Uncompahgre Plateau, 58, 112
Utah juniper, 50

Vail, 88, 112
Vail Nature Center, 117
Virginia's warbler, 63, 71
voles, 23

Walden, 59, 112
waterfall, 97
Watermelon Day, Arkansas Valley Fair, 117
watermelon snow, 102
wax currant, 80
weasels, 52
western bluebird, 81
western meadowlark, 31
western rattlesnake, 30, 41

western spotted skunk, 71
western tanager, 52, 81
western terrestrial garter snake, 61
western wheatgrass, 30
wheat, 26, 67
white fir, 52
White Ranch State Park, 73
White River, 58
White River National Forest, 88
white-crowned sparrow, 101
white-tailed deer, 61
white-tailed ptarmigan, 101, 103, 105, 106, 111
wild (Woods') rose, 90
wild turkey, 71, 73
Wilderness On Wheels, 117
wildflowers, 59, 72, 94–95, 104–105, 107, 109, 109, 115, 116
Williams Fork River, 53
Williamson's sapsucker, 81
willow, 52, 60, 102, 110
wolverine, 83
wolves, 26
Woodhouse's toad, 60
woodnymph, 90
woodpeckers, 83
woodrats, 43

yellow warbler, 61
yellow-bellied marmot, 101, 103, 104, 105, 111
yellow-rumped warbler, 91
yucca, 18, 22, 30